Ω Ω Ω Ω Ω Ω Ω Ω Ω Ω Ω Ω Ω Ω Ω Ω Ω Ω Ω Ω
Ω Ω Ω Ω Ω Ω Ω Ω Ω Ω Ω Ω Ω Ω Ω Ω Ω Ω Ω

MAURICE'S STRATEGIKON

Ω Ω Ω Ω Ω Ω Ω Ω Ω Ω Ω Ω Ω Ω Ω Ω Ω Ω Ω
Ω Ω Ω Ω Ω Ω Ω Ω Ω Ω Ω Ω Ω Ω Ω Ω Ω Ω Ω

THE MIDDLE AGES SERIES
Ruth Mazo Karras, Series Editor
Edward Peters, Founding Editor

A complete list of books in the series is available from
the publisher.

Ω Ω Ω Ω Ω Ω Ω Ω Ω Ω Ω Ω Ω Ω Ω Ω Ω Ω Ω Ω
Ω Ω Ω Ω Ω Ω Ω Ω Ω Ω Ω Ω Ω Ω Ω Ω Ω Ω Ω

MAURICE'S STRATEGIKON

HANDBOOK · OF BYZANTINE MILITARY STRATEGY

TRANSLATED BY
GEORGE T. DENNIS

UNIVERSITY OF PENNSYLVANIA PRESS
PHILADELPHIA

10 9 8 7 6 5 4 3

Published by
University of Pennsylvania Press
Philadelphia, Pennsylvania 19104-4011
ISBN 0-8122-1772-1

Library of Congress Cataloging-in-Publication Data

Strategikon. English.
    Maurice's Strategikon; transmitted under the name of a certain
Maurikios, attributed by some to Maurice, Emperor of the East; it
may have been written by Orbicius or by a certain Rufus—Cf. Pauly-
Wissowa; K. Krumbacher. Geschichte der byzantinischen Literatur, 2
Aufl. p. 635.
    Bibliography: p.
    Index.
    1. Military art and science— Handbooks, manuals, etc.
I. Maurikios. II. Maurice, Emperor of the East, 539–602.
III. Orbicius. IV. Rufus. V. Dennis, George T. VI. Title
VII. Title: Byzantine military strategy.
U101.S8413   1984   355'.002'02   83-10590

Ω Ω Ω Ω Ω Ω Ω Ω Ω Ω Ω Ω Ω Ω Ω Ω Ω Ω Ω Ω
Ω Ω Ω Ω Ω Ω Ω Ω Ω Ω Ω Ω Ω Ω Ω Ω Ω Ω Ω Ω

·CONTENTS·

Ω Ω Ω Ω Ω Ω Ω Ω Ω Ω Ω Ω Ω Ω Ω Ω Ω Ω Ω
Ω Ω Ω Ω Ω Ω Ω Ω Ω Ω Ω Ω Ω Ω Ω Ω Ω Ω Ω

·INTRODUCTION·

Between the beginning of the fourth century and the beginning of the seventh completely unforeseen and irreversible changes took place in what was thought to be the civilized world. Around the Mediterranean, into Europe and into Africa, one empire had held sway. From Scotland to Syria one political and legal system had dominated. In theory there were no states or nations. There was simply Rome and non-Rome. There was the civilized world, and there were the barbarians. Law and order were maintained and enemies held in check by one of the most efficient military machines in history, the Roman legion. Combining strength and flexibility, the legions were constantly on the march, building fortified camps, defending and expanding the boundaries of the empire with pickax and shovel as much as with sword and spear.

By the beginning of the seventh century all this had changed drastically. Germanic kings ruled in the West. The empire's center of gravity had moved off to the East. The lands around the eastern Mediterranean were able to deal with the invasions and had survived. The emperor and the civil servants resided in New Rome, Constantinople. Instead of Latin, Greek was spoken, and everyone was at least nominally Christian. The empire was half the size it had been, and would soon be reduced by half again. Still, its citizens called themselves Romans and would continue to do so for almost a thousand years. To them, apart from a temporary loss of some territory, the empire had not changed, indeed it could not and would not. God would not permit it. All remained the same, yet it was all different.

As the institutions and the physical appearance of the empire changed, so did its army. This was a period of transition in military

vii

history. Warfare as practiced in the ancient world underwent a series of transformations not unlike those introduced by the use of gunpowder a millennium later. The tough, disciplined legionary who, covered by his shield, used his short sword to cut his way through all opposition, and who could hold his ground against the wildest charge of Pict, Celt, or German, no longer corresponded to the needs of the time. Instead of fighting on foot, the legions mounted horses and became archers and lancers. As with their armament, the size of the units, tactics, all underwent significant changes.

In the course of the third and fourth centuries the legions came to be reduced in size, and a large number of new units were created. More emphasis was placed on mobility, and thus on cavalry, who could move more rapidly from one threatened frontier to another. The enemies of the Romans were also depending more and more on horses in their attacks. The Gothic tribes who had settled in the steppes north of the Black Sea had turned to riding horses and found that with good armament they could fight their battles more effectively.

Although many other factors were involved, the Gothic cavalry played a significant role in the battle of Adrianople on 9 August 378.[1] The huge Roman army, mostly infantry, under the personal command of the emperor Valens was assaulting the barricaded camp of the Goths when suddenly the Gothic horsemen came up and charged into the left flank of the Romans. They drove it in upon the center with such impact that the legions were pushed together so tightly that the men were unable to raise their swords and spears. Some 40,000 men, including the emperor and his chief officers, are said to have been killed. It was, according to the contemporary historian Ammianus Marcellinus, the worst defeat suffered by a Roman army in 500 years.

It was not long before the victors at Adrianople were being hired to serve in the Roman army. Instead of organizing new units, the emperors came to enlist Teutonic chieftains with their followers. Peoples bound by treaty, *Federati*, had been employed by Rome before, but not in such numbers. These war bands owed their allegiance to their leaders and were not part of the regular Roman army and did not observe its discipline. Reliance on groups of Germanic,

1. See T. Burns, "The Battle of Adrianople: A Reconsideration," *Historia. Zeitschrift für Alte Geschichte* 22 (1973): 336–45.

and then Hunnish, warriors, all horsemen, marked a break with Roman military tradition.

In the western part of the empire the Roman army disintegrated and was gradually replaced by the private armies of great landowners or those of Germanic warlords. In the East the army, as other institutions, continued in being but was profoundly transformed. The period in which this transformation occurred, however, is one in which there is an unfortunate gap in our historical sources. Reliable information about the middle and late fifth century is not plentiful, and the army which emerges after that is very different from what it had been.

The eastern half of the empire had been badly shaken by Germanic invaders, Huns, and Isaurians; religious controversies rankled, and the Persians were still a menace. But its larger population, its greater economic resources, its prosperous municipal life, and its solid administrative structure helped it to weather the series of crises which had submerged the West. The concept of one empire persisted, though, and it was the emperor's duty to make that concept a reality. Emperor Justinian, in particular, directed all his energies toward achieving that goal.

Justinian played a leading role in the government during his uncle Justin's reign (518–27) and ruled by himself to 565. The restoration of the universal Roman Empire animated his every move. This obviously included the recovery of the western lands occupied by Germanic tribes. The talented general Belisarius sailed to Africa in 533 with a force of 18,000 troops, and within a year secured the submission of the Vandals. In 535 he began what would become a twenty years' war against the Ostrogoths in Italy. Eventually the Byzantine armies under the command of Narses completed the subjugation of the country. A section of Spain was also reconquered, and for a while the Mediterranean almost became a Roman lake again.

While the credit for these impressive achievements belongs to the efficient management of Justinian and to some outstanding generals, mention must be made of their choice of armament and tactics. In the course of the fifth century these had evolved and improved. The Romans learned from their enemies, Teutonic or Persian, and turned their weapons against them. The Roman soldier in Justinian's time usually fought on horseback. Protected by his helmet and by mail, lamellar, or scale armor, he carried bow and arrow and a sword or else spear and shield. In the first chapter of his history of Justinian's wars, Procopius proudly pictures the cavalryman with a quiver of arrows hanging from his right side, a sword from his left, and sometimes with a spear on his back, riding along at full speed firing arrows with great force in all directions. It was not only a successful military system which assured those latter-day Romans of victory, but one which they believed was a decided improvement upon the venerable legions of their ancestors. Again Procopius, who has nothing but admiration for the armies of Justinian, derides those who did not share that admiration, "who reverence and worship the ancient times and give no credit to modern improvements."

The combination of mounted archer and lancer proved very effective, especially against foes who made use of only one or the other. The Romans could also employ either light or heavy cavalry, depending on the tactics of the ethnic group from which they hired their mercenaries. They had a greater variety of resources on which to draw, and in warfare they could display more versatility than other peoples. But such a variegated composition of the army contained serious disadvantages as well and posed a constant threat. The basic loyalty of the troops was more often directed to their immediate commander, whether a Roman general, such as Belisarius or Narses, or a Teutonic chieftain.

These problems became more serious toward the end of Justinian's reign, and critical in the decades following it. Moreover, old enemies, such as the Persians, were adopting heavier armor and weapons. The stirrup was coming into use, and this gave the cavalryman greater stability in the saddle and more force to his spear thrust. New enemies were attacking in the North, the Slavs and the Avars. The military organization of the empire began to crumble.

The conquests of Justinian, impressive though they were, had been purchased at a tremendous price in money and energy. Except for North Africa, most of them proved to be ephemeral. Only three years after Justinian's death the Lombards invaded Italy and soon had control of most of the country. More serious, however, was the fact that warfare in the West had meant neglect of the more important frontiers to the North and the East. It was the threat from those directions that Byzantium had to fear.

To free troops for his western expeditions, Justinian had to agree to pay tribute and to make a number of concessions to the Persians, although that did not prevent them from ravaging Roman territory on occasion. When Justinian's successor, Justin II (565–78), decided not to pay the tribute, war broke out and dragged on for some twenty years without either side gaining a clear victory. Most of it was fought over Armenia, which both states coveted for strategic and economic reasons. For the Byzantines, in addition, a good source of mercenaries had dried up when the Germanic peoples migrated elsewhere. They were coming to rely more and more on the Armenians for soldiers, and could not allow their land to fall under Persian rule. Internal troubles in Persia finally solved the problem for the Byzantines. The emperor Maurice (582–602) was able to carry the war to a successful conclusion, and in 591 arranged for a peace treaty in which the Persians yielded much of their Armenian conquests to Byzantium.

In the Balkan peninsula the situation could be considered even more serious. Early in Justinian's reign Slavic tribes began wandering and raiding across the Danube into the Balkans. It was not long before one of the nomadic peoples of Asia, the Avars, arrived and established a loose sort of empire in East Central Europe. The Avars, who are mentioned several times in the *Strategikon*, easily asserted their authority over the Slavs, and then turned their attention toward the Byzantine borders. In 582, the year of Maurice's accession to the throne, they seized the important fortified city of Sirmium and, with the Slavs, laid waste the entire Balkan peninsula. In the next few years Thessalonica was attacked twice. Far more ominous, though, was the fact that the Slavs were no longer content with raiding, but were settling themselves permanently on Byzantine land.

Maurice could do little against the Slavs until he had brought the Persians under control, and it was not until 592 that he commenced large-scale operations against them. Several times the Byzantine army crossed the Danube and defeated the Slavs and Avars. But there were simply too many of them in those remote and hostile regions, and the campaigns dragged on. The soldiers became discouraged at continuing a war they could not win. In 602, when ordered to spend the winter north of the Danube, they revolted, marched on Constantinople, overthrew Maurice, and proclaimed the half-barbarian Phokas as emperor. Without opposition the Slavs then continued their occupation of the Balkans.

Although he failed to contain the Slavic invaders, Maurice may well be regarded as one of the outstanding Byzantine rulers. He still thought in terms of a universal Roman Empire, and he reorganized the territories remaining in the West along military lines. The exarchates of Ravenna in Italy and Carthage in Africa were formed. This conjoining of civil and military authority would soon be extended to the provinces in Byzantium's heartland, Asia Minor and Greece. The system would prove fundamental to the prosperity of the Byzantine state for several centuries to come. The reign of Maurice, in the words of George Ostrogorsky, "marks an important step forward in the transformation of the worn out late Roman Empire into the new and vigorous organization of the medieval Byzantine Empire." [2]

Maurice's most important accomplishment was probably his reform of the Roman army. For this he was eminently well prepared, bringing with him a wealth of personal experience gained in the Balkans and on the eastern frontiers. He was a very practical man and knew what was needed. Much, if not most, of the weaponry and tactics which had developed since Adrianople was retained or improved. Contemporary historians mention Maurice's reforms but do not furnish many details, although they do make it clear that he became very unpopular among the soldiers. We are not sure which changes should be ascribed to Maurice; some may have been made before his time, some later. But he does seem to deserve credit for regularizing the changes and reorganizing the army as a whole along new lines. The reformed army of Maurice is the one described in the Handbook of Strategy (*Strategikon*) attributed to him. Some further changes would be made by Heraclius (610–41), or at least credited to him, or by later emperors. Improvements and adaptations would occur in armament and tactics. The army, though, which would preserve the Roman-Byzantine Empire into the tenth century and beyond remained much the same as that organized and described by Maurice.

Maurice did his best to put an end to the system of semiprivate armies which had prevailed for a century or more. Superior officers were to be appointed by the imperial government. The soldiers were to serve under delegates of the emperor instead of more or less independent warlords. The army was at the service of the state, not its commanders; it had become a national, an imperial, army.

The army's organization was also made more uniform, and it acquired greater unity and cohesion. For several reasons, the number

2. *History of the Byzantine State*, trans. J. Hussey (New Brunswick, N.J., 1969), 80.

of foreign mercenaries had dwindled, and those who were recruited could more easily be fitted into the Byzantine military structure. The basic unit of this structure, for both infantry and cavalry, was the bandon or tagma, a company of about three hundred soldiers. A number of these, as explained in the *Strategikon*, were then incorporated into larger divisions to form an army under the command of a general.

The military system elaborated by Maurice was a very well-organized one, so well organized, in fact, that it remained virtually unchanged for more than three hundred years. When the emperor Leo VI compiled his *Tactical Constitutions* around the beginning of the tenth century, he had little to add to Maurice's organization. Apart from some changes in terminology, Leo's chapters on armament and the organization of the troops are almost identical with those of Maurice.

Along with the famous and successful formations of antiquity, the Macedonian phalanx and the Roman legion, should be listed the Byzantine bandon. The word itself was Germanic, and it signified both the unit and the flag or banner which served as an identifying and rallying point for the soldiers. The unit was also called by the Greek word, *tagma*, a formation, or by the Latin *numerus*, a number (of troops), *arithmos* in Greek. Maurice clearly wanted the army to be recruited from among native Romans, whom we might now call Byzantines, although he makes allowances for foreigners. Probably a large percentage of the soldiers were natives. But as time went on the army came to be composed heavily of Armenians, as well as Slavic and Saracen prisoners of war.

The most perfect organization and equipment, however, depend on human beings to function properly, and the Byzantine army was no exception. The imperial bureaucracy might be late or default on paying the troops, and poor morale might lead them to desert or mutiny. There might be jealousy or corruption among the officers. Commanders might be cowardly or negligent. Many factors could and did lead to the defeat of a Byzantine army in the course of its history. But when the Byzantine commanders observed the regulations and instructions laid down in their manuals, they were generally assured of victory.

The basic reasons for the success of the Byzantine armies have been succinctly pointed out by Charles Oman. "In courage they

were equal to their enemies; in discipline, organization, and armament, far superior."[3] To this one could add that they inherited the
long tradition of Roman tactics and strategy with its emphasis on
constant adaptation to the changing exigencies of war. It was largely
this remarkable ability to adapt to new situations and new peoples
which guaranteed Byzantine military success.

The Byzantines, moreover, like the Romans, took warfare very
seriously. For them it was not a means of expansion and exploitation,
a demonstration of one's superiority, or a contest which would bring
the players glory and renown. For the Romans and for the Byzantines war was one of the means which the state might employ to
achieve its goals, and it was the least desirable of those means. Diplo-
macy, bribery, trickery were preferable. It was often less expensive
and risky to hire one barbarian tribe to fight another than to have the
Roman army march out to the uncertainties of combat. Even when
the decision had been made to go to war, the Byzantines, as much as
possible, tried to avoid actual combat and to rely on adroit maneuvering and strategems to achieve their goals.

For the Byzantines war was an art to be practiced by profes-
sionals. They possessed books on all aspects of warfare, which were
collected, copied over and over again, and presumably read. The fact
that officers in the Byzantine army had to be able to read and write
by itself sets it apart from other medieval armies. Byzantine generals
carefully studied the habits and tactics of their enemies, whereas
western knights found themselves at a loss when facing unknown
foes. The western European considered himself a good warrior if he
could ride and wield his weapons well and if he showed no fear. For
the Byzantine it was not superior strength or courage which won
battles but, after God's favor, thorough planning and intelligence.
Nothing should be left to chance. Maurice twice reminds his readers
that the Byzantine general should never have to admit: "I did not
expect that."

Serious writing in Greek about tactics and strategy had a long
tradition, of which the Byzantines believed they were an integral
part. The oldest extant work, however, belongs to the fourth century
B.C.E., a treatise by Aeneas the Tactician on what to do when besieged. He was followed by a steady stream of writings on almost

3. *The Art of War in the Middle Ages*, rev. ed. (Ithaca, N.Y., 1953), 32–33. This
statement needs serious qualification, however; see, for example, W. Kaegi,
Byzantine Military Unrest, 471–843: An Interpretation (Amsterdam, 1981).

every aspect of tactics, strategy, and military technology. Excerpts on
such topics as archery, sending secret messages, and siege machines
were published separately. Collections, compilations, and adaptations were made. The Byzantines, then, inherited a considerable library of books on military matters. And they continued to add to it,
especially in the sixth century, and then later in the tenth.[4] For the
sixth century there are works by Urbikios, Syrianos, and an anonymous one on military science probably dating to Justinian's reign.
Some simply repeat or paraphrase ancient authors. Some are very
theoretical, apparently composed by armchair strategists who never
saw a battlefield. There are also a few eminently practical works,
among which is the one attributed to emperor Maurice.

The military handbook (*strategikon*, *taktika*), which most manuscripts assign to Maurice, was intended for the average commanding
officer and was written in a language he could understand.[5] Although
it includes some general maxims and references to previous tactical
authors, the *Strategikon* is an original work without any literary pre-
tensions. The author, it is clear, was an experienced soldier who had
commanded troops on at least two fronts. While certainly an edu-
cated man, he uses common, everyday words and military terms,
even slang. His explanations are clear, complete, and illustrated by
diagrams. He knows and cites military law, and he refers to historical
precedents. He is familiar with the weapons, armor, and other
equipment actually in use. He is well acquainted with the daily life of
the soldier, on the march and in camp. As a veteran campaigner, he
knows the enemy and how he fights.

The *Strategikon* is an important piece of Byzantine writing, well
worth studying. Apart from the developing forms of Greek, the phi-
lologist may find clear evidence of the absorption of Latin, Germanic,
and words from other languages into the Greek military and administrative vocabulary. The book contains firsthand information about

4. See H. Hunger, *Die hochsprachliche profane Literatur der Byzantiner* (Munich,
1978), 2:323–40; A. Dain, "Les stratégistes byzantins," *Travaux et Mémoires*
2 (1967): 317–92.

5. See Hunger, *Die hochsprachliche profane Literatur*, 329–30; Dain, "Les Stratégistes," 344–46; G. Moravcsik, *Byzantinoturcica* (Berlin, 1958), 1:417–21;
F. Aussaresses, *L'Armée byzantine à la fin du VI siècle d'après le Stratégicon de
l'empereur Maurice* (Bordeaux, 1909); John Wiita, "The Ethnika in Byzantine
Military Treatises" (Ph.D. diss., University of Minnesota, 1977); G. Dennis, ed., *Das Strategikon des Maurikios*, Corpus fontium historiae byzantinae,
17 (Vienna, 1981): 13–18.

the characteristics of various peoples, Persians, Slavs, and others. The actual organization, armament, and tactics of the armies of the period are accurately presented. Scholars should be able to learn a great deal from this simple handbook. That the Byzantines themselves regarded the work as important is clear from the fact that they rewrote sections, and they used it as the basis for a series of adaptations and paraphrases. It even influenced reforms in western European armies as late as the beginning of the seventeenth century.[6]

Scholars are generally agreed that the *Strategikon* was composed between 575, when hostilities were renewed with the Persians, and 628, when they were finally defeated. Other enemies of the Byzantine Empire named in the text are the Lombards, who appear after 568, the Avars and the Slavs, who caused trouble in the mid-570s, and the Antes, about whom nothing is recorded after 601. Three recent events are mentioned in the *Strategikon*. The first is the poisoning of the barley for the horses by the Persians, which could refer to an order of Khusrau II in 591. Second, there is a reference to the siege of Aqbas in 583. Third, the author describes a stratagem employed by the Avars at Heracleia, which can be dated to 592. The invocation of the "Holy Trinity, our God and Savior," which is found at the beginning of the *Strategikon*, was regularly used to introduce imperial documents from 605 or earlier. Everything considered, it is reasonable to conclude that the *Strategikon* was composed during the latter part of the reign of Maurice (after 592) or during that of Phokas (before 610).[7]

The identity of the author of the *Strategikon* has not been clearly established. The principal manuscript attributes the work to Urbikios, an amateur tactician and poet in the time of Anastasius I (491–518), but this could be a simple scribal error, *urbikios* for [*M*]*aurikios*. The other manuscripts and later writers ascribe the work to Emperor Maurice. The Ambrosian codex entitles the book: "The Taktika of Maurice who lived during the reign of Emperor Maurice." The Greek could originally have read: "The Taktika of Maurice who later became Emperor Maurice." As pointed out above, Maurice had had extensive military experience in the East against the Persians and along the Danube against the Slavs, as the author of the *Strategikon* had also certainly had, and he was interested

6. Wiita, "Ethnika," 11.
7. Details and references in Dennis, *Das Strategikon*, and Wiita, "Ethnika."

in the organization of the army and its tactics. Long ago F. Aussaresses concluded that although the emperor's authorship cannot be
categorically proven, all the evidence is clearly in favor of it.[8]

More recently John Wiita has proposed that the treatise may have
been written by Philippicus, general and brother-in-law of Maurice.[9]
He seems to have served with Maurice on the eastern frontier in
577–82, and in 583 became supreme commander in those regions
(*magister militum per orientem*). He accumulated some wealth and built
a monastery and villa near Constantinople. Although not consistently successful on the battlefield, he had good rapport with his
officers and troops. An experienced and cautious general, he was
noted for his study of history and the characteristics of other nations.
He had a special interest in Hannibal, which is of some relevance,
since two of the half-dozen or so anecdotes in the book concern him.
In short, he possessed the qualities found in the author of the *Strategikon*. He was forced to spend the years 603–610 in a monastery,
which would have given him the opportunity for reflection, research, and writing. He died about 615.

In the ancient and medieval worlds, of course, naming an emperor as author of a work does not necessarily mean that he took pen
in hand and actually wrote out the words. It could, and often enough
did, mean that the work was composed and written at his orders or
under his direction. Such could be the case with Maurice and his
Handbook. Still, there are so many personal touches that one becomes almost convinced that the work was planned and written
directly by an experienced military commander, a general or an emperor. Whether this person was Emperor Maurice is a question to
which no unqualified answer can be given.

The original *Strategikon* consisted of the first eleven books, for the
author explicitly concluded his work at the end of Book XI. The
general index at the beginning may have been compiled by the author, and the introduction too was probably composed by him and
included in the original work, for in style and content it clearly forms
an integral part of the text. Book XII, or most of it, was added later,
but not much later, and certainly by the author himself. In explaining
the articles of war to the infantry he states: ". . . as we mentioned in
the treatise on the cavalry."

8. "L'auteur de Stratégicon," *Revue des études anciennes* 8 (1906): 23–40.
9. "Ethnika," 30–49.

The twelfth book comprises four more or less autonomous sections of unequal length and importance. A fifth, the *Epitedeuma* of Urbikios, was added to the second manuscript family at a later date. It is not in the principal manuscripts and is extraneous in style and content, and has not been included in the most recent edition or this translation. The second of the sections in Book XII is a treatise or small book in itself on the infantry. It may have been an earlier work adapted, perhaps somewhat revised, by the author and incorporated into the *Strategikon*. The style resembles that of the first eleven books, but there are enough differences, especially in the last chapter, to postulate an independent origin. It contains many reminders of the Justinianic armies, such as Gothic shoes, Herulian swords, and Moorish javelins. The putative enemies are the Scythians, Slavs, Antes, and Persians, and the herald is required to speak Persian. The third section consists of one page with a diagram of a fortified camp, which is extant only in the Ambrosian manuscript, although it was once in the Laurentian, for there are dots tracing the camp's outline on the next folio.

The text of the *Strategikon* does not seem to have been copied many times.[10] It was written toward the end of a flourishing period of literary and technical writing and just before a period, a dark age, in which it seems that very little writing was done and very few manuscripts were copied. From roughly 650 to 800 the production of books of all sorts declined noticeably. Upon completing his work, the author must have had a few copies made. At least three copies were produced in the first half of the seventh century, and these gave rise to the three families of manuscripts which have transmitted the text to us. Sometime, perhaps early in the ninth century, manuscripts of each family were transliterated from uncial to minuscule script, and eventually further copies were made, continuing the three families or textual traditions.

The first family, which A. Dain calls the "authentic" recension, survives in a manuscript in the Laurentian Library in Florence, *codex Mediceo-Laurentianus graecus 55, 4.* Although several pages are missing, this is still a large book, 404 folios, clearly and neatly written on good parchment. It was copied about the middle of the tenth century as one volume of the encyclopedic production directed by Emperor

10. The history of the text is discussed in detail by Dennis, *Das Strategikon*, 28–42.

Constantine VII Porphyrogenitus and was apparently intended as the official edition of military writings to be deposited in the imperial library. It later came into the possession of Demetrius Laskaris Leontares, a general and military aide of Emperor Manuel II Palaeologus, who made use of the blank spaces to record births and deaths in his family from 1408 to 1439. His grandson, also Demetrius, made some additional notations in 1448–50. The volume was purchased by Janus Laskaris in Thessaly in 1491 and brought to Florence.

The book contains three distinct strategical collections: the first is of strategists of the Byzantine period, including the present *Strategikon*, the second of those of antiquity, and the third consists mostly of works of Emperor Leo VI. Of the extant manuscripts, this is clearly the closest to the original work, separated from it by no more than three or four copies. The diagrams are generally more accurate than in the other families, and the military commands, mostly written in Greek letters, conform more exactly to the original Latin.

The second family or recension, which Dain calls "interpolated," survives in three manuscripts, now located in Rome, Naples, and Paris, but which were copied in the same scriptorium in Constantinople in the first half of the eleventh century. These three are further removed from the original text than is the Laurentian one. They have more than twice as many errors and omissions, and they also contain a number of interpolations, glosses, and additions, probably incorporated at an early period.

The third manuscript tradition can be only partially reconstituted from its two surviving witnesses, both of which are compositions of Emperor Leo VI (886–912). The *Problemata* is a sort of military catechism. The author asks a question and replies by citing the text of the *Strategikon*, generally verbatim. Leo VI later attempted to compose an original work by arranging older material, including the *Strategikon*, according to a logical plan. The resultant treatise, *Tactical Constitutions*, is divided into twenty books, exists in three redactions, and was copied more than any other Byzantine military work.

Another version of the *Strategikon*, actually a paraphrase in contemporary Greek, is found in the Ambrosian Library in Milan. Written about the year 959, it does not fit clearly into the tradition. Its scribe used manuscripts of the first and second families as the basis for his edition, but he made use of a manuscript, now lost, of the same age or older than the Laurentian. As a result, this version has preserved several correct readings in places where the other manu-

scripts are wrong or missing. Its reproduction of the diagrams, especially in Book XII, is often more accurate and complete.

The first printed edition of the *Strategikon* was by Johann Scheffer
of Strasbourg: Joannes Schefferus, *Arriani Tactica et Mauricii Artis militaris libri duodecim* (Uppsala, 1664). Lucas Holste, the librarian of
Cardinal Francesco Barberini, had collated the text from four manuscripts and sent it to Scheffer, who made some changes, translated it
into Latin, and added some comments. The text is based on the second manuscript family and contains a number of errors. In his in-
complete edition of the *Tactical Constitutions* of Leo VI, the Hungarian
scholar, R. Vári, edited some sections of the *Strategikon*, but his work
is of limited value. The edition by H. Mihăescu, *Mauricius Arta militară*
(Bucharest, 1970), which includes a Rumanian translation, some
notes, and an index, was an improvement, but is subject to criticism
on a number of grounds.

In the 1920s Colonel, later General, Oliver L. Spaulding, Jr., of the
United States Army, began work on an English translation of the
Strategikon, using the Scheffer text. In 1935, while an instructor in
military science at Harvard University, he submitted his translation,
together with some notes, to the Medieval Academy of America. It
was suggested that he compare the Greek text with the Laurentian
and other manuscripts and make the necessary revisions. Colonel
Spaulding then contacted Professor Martin R. P. McGuire of the
Catholic University of America in Washington and proposed that he
aid in preparing a critical edition of the Greek text. Not long after-
wards, Dr. McGuire, with Colonel Spaulding's agreement, invited
the Reverend Martin J. Higgins, also a professor at Catholic University, to collaborate with him. A few years later, administrative duties
compelled Dr. McGuire to relinquish his part in the project, and
Monsignor Higgins assumed sole responsibility. He made an exhaus-
tive study and collation of the manuscripts and comparisons of the
diagrams. As it stands, his edition consists of a typed text and translation in parallel columns, with a listing of variants and conjectures
written by hand on facing pages. Apparently it was nearing completion in 1964, but Monsignor Higgins soon became seriously ill and
was unable to continue the work. One of the binders contains a note
in his hand which reads: "These three vols. contain various studies of
variants. (Probably will never have time to continue.) June 4, 1968."
He died the following year, 22 April 1969. General Spaulding had
died in 1947. His translation shows a number of revisions, presum-

ably made by Higgins. It is a free translation, and its accuracy on
many points may be questioned. It has, nonetheless, been helpful in
the preparation of the present translation.

The basic importance of the text and the amount of labor already
expended on it dictated that the work begun by Higgins and Spaulding be brought to completion. The present writer undertook this
task, beginning serious work on the Greek text in the spring of 1975.
About the same time, John E. Wiita was engaged in research for his
doctoral dissertation on Book XI of the *Strategikon* (University of
Minnesota, 1977), and made some significant contributions to the
project. The edition of the Greek text with critical apparatus, introduction, indices, and German translation has now appeared: *Das
Strategikon des Maurikios*, ed. George Dennis, trans. Ernst Gamillscheg,
Corpus fontium historiae byzantinae 17 (Vienna, 1981). It is on this
text that the English translation presented here is based.[11]

The *Strategikon* is written in a very straightforward and generally
uncomplicated Greek. The translation has tried to render this in the
same kind of English. Some words which have no exact equivalent in
English or which would be awkward if translated literally have been
left in Greek or near-Greek: e.g. *foulkon*, *tagma*, *pentarch*, *merarch*. This
is particularly true of the names for units and officers of the Byzantine army. Company or regiment are not exactly the same as *tagma* or
meros; a *merarch* is not really a colonel. In such cases the Greek terms
have generally been retained. One exception is the plural of *meros*;
divisions seems preferable to *mere* or *meroses*. In the original text
words of command were given in Latin, generally in Greek letters;
here they have been translated into English, with the Latin given in
a note.

11. Apart from Scheffer's Latin and Mihăescu's Rumanian translations, there is
a Russian one by K. Tsybyshev, *Mavrikii Taktika i Strategija* (St. Petersburg,
1903), and two in French, both unpublished, cited by Dain, "Les Stratégistes," 344.

Ω Ω Ω Ω Ω Ω Ω Ω Ω Ω Ω Ω Ω Ω Ω Ω Ω Ω Ω Ω Ω
Ω Ω Ω Ω Ω Ω Ω Ω Ω Ω Ω Ω Ω Ω Ω Ω Ω Ω Ω Ω Ω

BIBLIOGRAPHICAL
NOTE

A very general picture of the age of transition from the ancient world to the Middle Ages is drawn by P. Brown, *The World of Late Antiquity A.D. 150–750* (London, 1971). E. Gibbon, *The Decline and Fall of the Roman Empire* (1776; edition with notes by J. B. Bury, 1896) still makes for pleasant reading but, especially in treating of the Byzantines, is full of prejudice and inaccuracies. More detailed and useful are the following: F. Lot, *The End of the Ancient World and the Beginnings of the Middle Ages*, trans. P. and M. Leon (New York, 1931); O. Seeck, *Geschichte des Untergangs der antiken Welt*, 6 vols. (Stuttgart, 1920–23); E. Stein, *Geschichte des spätrömischen Reiches*, vol. 1 of *Vom römischen zum byzantinischen Staate (284–476)* (Vienna, 1928; French trans., 2 vols., Paris, 1959); *De la disparition de l'Empire d'Occident à la mort de Justinien (476–565)*, vol. 2 of *Histoire du Bas-Empire* (Paris, 1949); A. H. M. Jones, *The Later Roman Empire, 284–602*, 2 vols. (Norman, Okla., 1964).

A broad view of the Byzantine Empire, including a brief chapter on its army, is found in C. Diehl, *Byzantium: Greatness and Decline*, trans. N. Walford (New Brunswick, N.J., 1957), with a bibliographical note by P. Charanis. More detailed are: J. M. Hussey et al., eds., *The Byzantine Empire*, vol. 4 of *The Cambridge Medieval History* (Cambridge, 1966–67); G. Ostrogorsky, *History of the Byzantine State*, trans. J. Hussey (New Brunswick, N.J., 1969).

For the period closer to the age of Emperor Maurice the following works are useful. J. B. Bury, *History of the Late Roman Empire from the Death of Theodosius I to the Death of Justinian*, 2 vols. (London, 1923); P. Goubert, *Byzance et l'Orient sous les successeurs de Justinien. L'empereur Maurice*, vol. 1 of *Byzance avant l'Islam* (Paris, 1953); B. Rubin, *Das Zeitalter Justinians I* (Berlin, 1960); A. N. Stratos, *Byzantium in the Seventh Century*, trans. M. Ogilvie-Grant and H. Hionides, 3 vols. (Amsterdam, 1968–72).

For a general view of medieval warfare, including the Byzantine, one may still consult the works of C. W. C. Oman, *The Art of War in the Middle Ages* (London, 1885; rev. ed. by J. Beeler, Ithaca, N.Y., 1953); *A*

History of the Art of War in the Middle Ages, 2 vols. (London, 1924); also F. Lot, *L'Art militaire au moyen âge en Europe et dans le Proche Orient*, 2 vols. (Paris, 1946). While a number of books treat of the old Roman army, e.g., M. Grant, *The Army of the Caesars* (London, 1974), very few pages are devoted to the Byzantine military. For the early period the basic work is still R. Grosse, *Römische militärgeschichte von Gallienus bis zum Beginn der byzantinischen Themenverfassung* (Berlin, 1920). Perhaps the most complete is L. Bréhier, *Les Institutions de l'empire byzantin* (Paris, 1949), 334–429. Chapter 22 of the *Cambridge Medieval History* cited above briefly discusses the Byzantine army, as do some of the other general works on Byzantine civilization. In Chapter 17 of *The Later Roman Empire* Jones treats of the administration and organization of the army up to the year 602 in some detail. More or less of a paraphrase of the *Strategikon* with some commentary is found in F. Aussaresses, *L'Armée byzantine à la fin du VI° siècle d'après le Stratégicon de l'empereur Maurice* (Bordeaux, 1909). One should also consult A. Pertusi, *Ordinamenti militari, guerre in Occidente e teoria di guerra dei bizantini (secc. vi–x)*, Settimane di Studi sull'alto medioevo, 15 (Spoleto, 1968): 631–700. C. Mazzucchi has compared the diagrams in the *Strategikon* with contemporary battle formations: "Le katagraphai dello Strategicon di Maurizio e lo schieramento di battaglia dell'esercito romano nel vi/vii secolo," *Aevum* 55 (1981): 111–38. Mention should also be made of two articles by V. Kuchma, "Vizantijskie voennye traktaty VI–X vv. kak istočniki po istorii voennogo iskusstva vizantijskij imperii," *Antičnaja drevnost i srednie veka. Učenye zapiski Uralskij gosudarstvennyj Universitet* 53 (1966): 31–56; "Vizantijskie voennye traktaty VI–X vv. kak istoričeskij istočnik," *Vizantijskij Vremennik* 40 (1979): 49–75.

While the study of Byzantine military organization and history would seem to be in its infancy, some solid research on specific topics has been carried on, as exemplified by the following. A. Bivar, "Cavalry Equipment and Tactics on the Euphrates Frontier," *Dumbarton Oaks Papers* 26 (1972): 271–91; J. Haldon, "Some Aspects of Byzantine Military Technology from the Sixth to the Tenth Century," *Byzantine and Modern Greek Studies* 1 (1975): 11–47; *Recruitment and Conscription in the Byzantine Army c. 530–950: A Study on the Origins of the Stratiotika Ktemata* (Vienna, 1979); W. E. Kaegi, "Some Reconsiderations on the Themes: Seventh–Ninth Centuries," *Jahrbuch der Österreichischen byzantinischen Gesellschaft* 16 (1967): 39–53; *Byzantine Military Unrest, 471–843: An Interpretation* (Amsterdam, 1981); G. Dennis, "Byzantine Battle Flags," *Byzantinische Forschungen* 8 (1981): 51–60; P. Schreiner, "Zur Ausrüstung des Kriegers in Byzanz, im Kiever Russland und in Nordeuropa nach bildlichen und literarischen Quellen," in *Les pays du Nord et Byzance*, ed. R. Zeitler (Uppsala, 1981), 215–36.

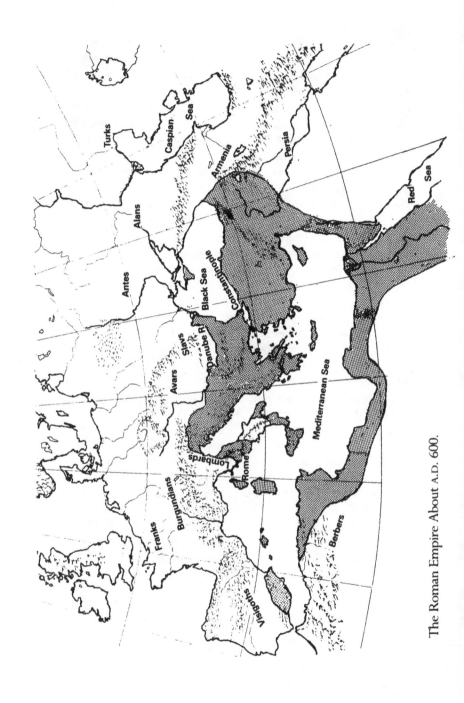

The Roman Empire About A.D. 600.

Ω Ω Ω Ω Ω Ω Ω Ω Ω Ω Ω Ω Ω Ω Ω Ω Ω Ω Ω
Ω Ω Ω Ω Ω Ω Ω Ω Ω Ω Ω Ω Ω Ω Ω Ω Ω Ω

MAURICE'S STRATEGIKON

Contents

1

C O N T E N T S

Book III · Formations of the Tagma   35

2

C O N T E N T S

3

CONTENTS

5

C O N T E N T S

6

CONTENTS

LET WORD AND DEED BE GUIDED BY THE ALL HOLY
Trinity, our God and Savior, the steadfast hope and assurance of divine assistance, who directs important and beneficial undertakings to
a favorable conclusion.[1] Well aware of our own weakness, we have
been motivated solely by devotion to the nation. If, then, what we
have written should be deficient, the Holy Trinity will put it in order,
turn it to our advantage, and provide guidance for those who may
read it. May this come about through the intercession of our Lady,
the immaculate, ever-virgin Mother of God, Mary, and of all the
saints, for blessed is our God for never-ending ages of ages. Amen.

The state of the armed forces has been neglected for a long time
and has fallen so completely into oblivion, so to speak, that those
who assume the command of troops do not understand even the
most obvious matters and run into all sorts of difficulties. Sometimes
the soldiers are blamed for lack of training, sometimes the generals
for inexperience. We have resolved, therefore, to do some writing on
this subject, as best we can, succinctly and simply, drawing in part
on ancient authors and in part on our limited experience of active
duty, with an eye more to practical utility than to fine words. In so
doing we make no pretense of breaking new ground or of trying to
improve upon the ancients. For they, in addressing their writings
to knowledgeable and experienced men, dealt with topics not readily
understood by laymen, and passed over basic, introductory matters,
which are particularly necessary nowadays. In our judgment, now, it
is essential not to overlook even the most obvious things, which are
fundamental if one is to command troops successfully. We have,
then, devised a rather modest elementary handbook or introduction
for those devoting themselves to generalship, which should facilitate
the progress of those who wish to advance to a better and more
detailed knowledge of those ancient tactical theories. For this reason,
as already remarked, we have paid no attention to the niceties of
graceful writing or fine-sounding words. This is not something sa-

1. Maurice had decreed that all imperial documents should begin: "In the
   name of our Lord Jesus Christ, our God and Savior." Then the Trinitarian
   formula came to be employed regularly, its first recorded use being in 605:
   see John Wiita, "The Ethnika in Byzantine Military Treatises" (Ph.D. diss.,
   University of Minnesota, 1977), 21.

cred we are doing. Our concern, rather, has been with practicality and brevity of expression. With this in mind, a good number of Latin terms and other expressions in ordinary military use have been employed to make it easier to understand the subject matter. If, then, anything useful be found in this composition, thanks be to Almighty God, who has favored us with some understanding of these matters. And if any general should through his own experience and diligence come to understand more about such matters, thanks be again to God, the giver of all good things, and may we, if we seem too enthusiastic, be judged leniently.

First, we urge upon the general that his most important concern be the love of God and justice; building on these, he should strive to win the favor of God, without which it is impossible to carry out any plan, however well devised it may seem, or to overcome any enemy, however weak he may be thought. For all things are ruled by the providence of God, a providence which extends even to the birds and the fishes. A helmsman, now, even the best, finds that his skill is useless when the winds are not blowing favorably, but when he has them with him and also puts his skill to use, he has no difficulty in doubling the ship's run. So it is with a good general. Armed with the favor of God and, without pausing to rest, employing his tactical and strategical skills, he manages the army entrusted to him with confidence and is able to counter the various machinations of the enemy. It is this which makes things turn out to one's advantage and which brings one's plans to a favorable conclusion. To those he deals with the general should appear calm and untroubled; his food and clothing should be plain and simple; his entourage should not be elaborate and ostentatious; he should be tireless and painstaking in attending to his duties, not slack or careless; care and persistence will easily carry him through the most difficult situations. If he shows no concern for a problem, that problem will show no concern for him.

He should often deliberate about his most serious problems and carry out what he has decided with as little delay and risk as possible. For opportunity is what cures problems. To his subordinates he should appear even-tempered. He ought not to be easy in dealing with those who have committed offenses out of cowardice or carelessness in the hope of being regarded as a good leader, for a good leader does not encourage cowardice and laziness. On the other hand, he ought not to punish hastily and without a full investigation just to show he can act firmly. The first leads to contempt and disobedience; the other to well-deserved hatred with all its consequences. Both of these are extremes. The better course is to join fear with justice, that is, impose a fitting punishment upon offenders after proof of guilt. This, for reasonable men, is not punishment, but correction, and aids in maintaining order and discipline.

· B O O K   I ·
Introduction

1. The Training and Drilling of the Individual Soldier

He should be trained to shoot rapidly on foot, either in the Roman or the Persian manner.[2] Speed is important in shaking the arrow loose and discharging it with force. This is essential and should also be practiced while mounted. In fact, even when the arrow is well aimed, firing slowly is useless. He should practice shooting rapidly on foot from a certain distance at a spear or some other target. He should also shoot rapidly mounted on his horse at a run, to the front, the rear, the right, the left. He should practice leaping onto the horse.[3] On horseback at a run he should fire one or two arrows rapidly and put the strung bow in its case, if it is wide enough, or in a half-case designed for this purpose, and then he should grab the spear which he has been carrying on his back. With the strung bow in its case, he should hold the spear in his hand, then quickly replace it on his back, and grab the bow. It is a good idea for the soldiers to practice all this while mounted, on the march in their own country. For such exercises do not interfere with marching and do not wear out the horses.

2. It seems that the Roman manner, taken from the steppe nomads, consisted of drawing the bowstring with thumb and forefinger, whereas the Persians did it with the lower three fingers: A. Bivar, "Cavalry Equipment and Tactics on the Euphrates Frontier," *Dumbarton Oaks Papers* 26 (1972): 285.
3. These exercises are mentioned by Vegetius, *Epitoma rei militaris*, 1, 18. The Life of St. Anastasius the Persian (martyred in 628) records that in March the soldiers were accustomed to equip their horses and train them for battle: *Acta S. Anastasii Persae*, ed. H. Usener, Programma Universitatis Bonnae (1884), 23.

2. The Armament of the Cavalryman and the Basic Equipment to Be Furnished

With individual training progressing satisfactorily, the soldiers must be armed by their commanding officers. The proper equipment needed on campaign may be gotten ready in the leisure of winter quarters. Each soldier should have the equipment corresponding to his rank and his pay and perquisites. This is especially true of the commanders of a meros, a moira, or a tagma, and of hekatontarchs, dekarchs, pentarchs, and tetrarchs, and of the bucellary and federate troops.[4] They should have hooded coats of mail reaching to their ankles, which can be caught up by thongs and rings, along with carrying cases; helmets with small plumes on top; bows suited to the strength of each man, and not above it, more in fact on the weaker side, cases broad enough so that when necessary they can fit the strung bows in them, with spare bow strings in their saddle bags; quivers with covers holding about thirty or forty arrows; in their baldrics small files and awls; cavalry lances of the Avar type with leather thongs in the middle of the shaft and with pennons; swords; round neck pieces of the Avar type made with linen fringes outside and wool inside. Young foreigners unskilled with the bow should have lances and shields. It is not a bad idea for the bucellary troops to make use of iron gauntlets and small tassels hanging from the back straps and the breast straps of the horses, as well as small pennons hanging from their own shoulders over the coats of mail. For the more handsome the soldier is in his armament, the more confidence he gains in himself and the more fear he inspires in the enemy.

Apart from the foreigners, all the younger Romans up to the age of forty must definitely be required to possess bow and quiver, whether they be expert archers or just average. They should possess two lances so as to have a spare at hand in case the first one misses.

---

4. The bucellary troops, *Bucellarii*, were originally soldiers employed by private individuals. Recruited from both Romans and barbarians, they came to form part of the regular army and eventually settled in the Boukellarion theme in Asia Minor. See A. H. M. Jones, *The Later Roman Empire, 284–602,* (Norman, Okla., 1964), 1: 665–68; *Costatino Porfirogenito De Thematibus,* ed. A. Pertusi, Studi e Testi 160 (Vatican City, 1952), 133–36.

The federate troops (*Federati*) began as allied tribes serving in accord with a treaty, but by the sixth century they had become simply barbarians enrolled in the regular army, a sort of foreign legion. See Jones, *Later Roman Empire,* 663–66.

Unskilled men should use lighter bows. Given enough time, even those who do not know how to shoot will learn, for it is essential that they do so.

The horses, especially those of the officers and the other special troops,[5] in particular those in the front ranks of the battle line, should have protective pieces of iron armor about their heads and breast plates of iron or felt, or else breast and neck coverings such as the Avars use.

The saddles should have large and thick cloths; the bridles should be of good quality; attached to the saddles should be two iron stirrups,[6] a lasso with thong, hobble, a saddle bag large enough to hold three or four days' rations for the soldier when needed. There should be four tassels on the back strap, one on top of the head, and one under the chin.

The men's clothing, especially their tunics, whether made of linen, goat's hair, or rough wool, should be broad and full, cut according to the Avar pattern, so they can be fastened to cover the knees while riding and give a neat appearance.

They should also be provided with an extra-large cloak or hooded mantle of felt with broad sleeves to wear, large enough to wear over their armament, including the coat of mail and the bow. Then, in case it should rain or be damp from the dew, by wearing this garment over the coat of mail and the bow they may protect their armament and still not find it awkward to use the bow or the lance. Such cloaks are also necessary in another way on patrol, for when the mail is covered by them, its brightness will not be seen at a distance by the enemy, and they also provide some protection against arrows.

Each squad should have a tent, as well as sickles and axes to meet any contingency. It is well to have the tents of the Avar type, which combine practicality with good appearance.[7]

The men, especially those receiving allowances for the purpose, should certainly be required to provide servants for themselves, slave or free, according to the regulations in force. At the time of distributing pay, care should be taken, just as with the soldiers, to register the servants and their arms, and inquiry should be made to know

5. That is, dekarch, pentarch, tetrarch, and the two file guards.
6. For stirrup Maurice uses the word *skala*, step or stair, for it had only recently come into use among the Byzantines and they did not have a special word for it.
7. The Avar tents were round and roomy.

under what sort of title they receive their pay. Should they neglect this and find themselves without servants, then in time of battle it will be necessary to detail some of the soldiers themselves to the baggage train, and there will be fewer fighting in the ranks. But if, as can easily happen, some of the men are unable to afford servants, then it will be necessary to require that three or four lower-ranking soldiers join in maintaining one servant. A similar arrangement should be followed for the pack animals, which may be needed to carry the coats of mail and the tents.

The fields of the flags in each meros should be of the same color, and the streamers in each moira should also have their own color, so that each individual tagma may easily recognize its own standard. Other distinctive devices known to the soldiers should be imposed on the fields of the flags, so that they may easily be recognized according to meros, moira, and tagma. The standards of the merarchs should be particularly distinctive and conspicuous, so they may be recognized by their troops at a great distance.[8]

The general must see that his baggage train carries extra arms, especially bows and arrows, to replace those weapons which are likely to be lost.

While in winter quarters, the commanders of the tagmas, if they cannot easily purchase supplies in the country, should ascertain their needs. They should then let the merarchs know how many horses and what sort of equipment and arms the troops under their command need, so that the general may make timely arrangements to purchase them for the soldiers.

Besides the leather cases for the coats of mail, they should have light wicker ones. During battle or on raids they may be carried behind the saddle arch by the horse's loins. Then if, as in the case of a reversal, the men with the spare horses are missing for a day, the coats of mail will not be left unprotected and ruined and the soldiers will not be worn out by the constant weight of the armor.

3. The Various Titles of the Officers and the Soldiers

Now that we have described the training of the individual soldier and his armament, we think we ought to explain the meaning of the

8. G. Dennis, "Byzantine Battle Flags," *Byzantinische Forschungen* 8 (1982): 51–59.

names of the officers, the units, and the other soldiers which form
part of a complete study of tactics. Our intention in doing this is to
give our readers a more accurate knowledge, so that on first hearing
such names they may not find that they do not know what they
mean.

First, the head and leader of the whole army is called the general;
the man who ranks second after him is the lieutenant general (*hypostrategos*). The merarch is the one entrusted with the command of a
meros; the moirarch is the commander of a moira and is called
a duke. A meros or division is an assemblage or grouping composed
of three moiras. A moira is made up of tagmas, arithmoi, or bandons.
A count or tribune commands the tagma, arithmos, or bandon.[9] Ilarch is the term for the first of the hekatontarchs, who is second in
command to the count or tribune. A hekatontarch commands a
hundred men, just as a dekarch is the leader of ten, and the pentarch
of five. The tetrarch, also known as the guard, is the leader of the rear
guard and the last in the file. The standard bearer carries the symbol of the bandon. Next in rank to him is the cape bearer.[10] The
moirarchs of the Optimates are referred to as taxiarchs.[11] The auxiliary soldier or shield bearer of one of the Optimates is called man-
at-arms.

Assault troops is the term used for those who move out ahead of
the main line and rush upon the retreating enemy.[12] Defenders are
those who follow them, not charging out or breaking ranks, but
marching in good order as a support for the assault troops if they
should happen to fall back.[13] Medical corpsmen is the name for those
who follow behind the line to rescue and take care of those wounded
in the battle.[14] Quartering parties are those troops who on the march
go ahead of the main column to reconnoiter and look for good roads
and places to pitch camp. Surveyors are those who measure and set

9. *Tagma* implies a group drawn up in order or in formation; *arithmos* (Latin
    numerus) means a number of troops; *bandon* is the word for a flag, extended
    to designate the unit serving under that flag.
10. Cape bearer: apparently an orderly.
11. Optimates: from Latin *optimus*, a body of troops formed in the late Roman
    Empire, probably around the end of the third century, which would even-
    tually settle in the theme of Optimaton in northwestern Asia Minor: Per-
    tusi, ed., *Costatino Porfirogenito De Thematibus*, 130–33.
12. Assault troops: *koursores* (Latin *cursores*), troops in open or extended order.
13. Defenders: *defensores*, troops in close order.
14. Medical corpsmen: *deputatoi* (Latin *deputati*).

15

up the camps. Spies are called scouts. Flank guards are those assigned
to guard the flanks of the first line. Outflankers are those who are
assigned to envelop the enemy wings. The baggage train consists of
the soldiers' supplies and includes servants, pack animals, and other
beasts.

4. The Organization of the Army and the Assignment of Officers

After the men have been armed according to regulations, and arrangements made for the necessary supplies for the army, and the
terms employed to designate the individual officers and men made
clear, the army must be divided into various units and commands,
and intelligent and competent officers placed over them.

Tagmas should be formed varying in strength from three hundred
to four hundred men at the most, and counts, also called tribunes,
prudent and competent, should be placed over them. The tagmas
should be organized into moiras or chiliarchies consisting of two or
three thousand men, depending on the size of the army, and placed
under the command of competent moirarchs, also called dukes or
chiliarchs, prudent and disciplined. These moiras then are grouped
into three equal meroses and over them are placed merarchs, also
called stratelates, prudent, practical, experienced, and, if possible,
able to read and write. This is especially important for the commander of the center meros, called lieutenant general, who has to, if
it becomes necessary, take over all the duties of the general.

The army, therefore, is organized as follows. First, the cavalrymen
are divided into various tagmas, the tagmas into moiras or chiliarchies, the moiras into three equal divisions, that is, center, right, left,
which comprise the battle line under command of the general. The
tagma should not exceed four hundred men, except in the bandons
of the Optimates, nor should the moira have more than three thousand, nor the meros more than six or seven thousand. In case the
army is larger than this, it is better to place the additional troops
outside the meros formation, to support the second line, to guard
the flanks and rear of the meros, and to ambush and encircle the
enemy. The meros or the moira should not be made too large. Otherwise, as they become larger and more extended, they may prove to
be disorderly and confused.

All of the tagmas should definitely not be of the same strength. If

they are, the enemy can easily estimate the size of the army by counting standards. Still, the statement we have made above should be
observed, that is, the tagma should not contain more than four hundred men or less than two hundred.

5. How the Tagmatic Commanders Should Select
Their Subordinate Officers and Combat Leaders
and Organize the Tagma into Squads

After the organization of the army, each commander must organize
and divide his own tagma into squads. First of all, from the whole
tagma he must select men of sound judgment and courage as hekatontarchs, taking particular care in choosing the ilarch, who is to
be second in command of the tagma. Then he should choose the
dekarchs, who should be courageous, good at hand-to-hand fighting and, if possible, good shots with the bow. Next are the pentarchs
and tetrarchs, whose qualifications should be similar. Finally, there
should be two additional men per squad to act as file guards, adding
up to five specially rated men in each file. The rest, both veterans and
recruits, should be assigned to squads. After he has taken care of
these, the commander should assign the specially rated troops according to the qualities of each, the best men first and then the others in relative order.

Two alert and intelligent men should be chosen as heralds, and
also two standard bearers. This sort of selection and assignment
should be made in the squads, that is, in the files. If there are no
servants, the poorer soldiers should be detailed to take care of the
pack animals, one man to three or four animals. Another man, a
competent one, should be taken from the regular soldiers and given a
standard, and the entire baggage train or pack animals should follow
him. Finally, the commander must determine how many and which
files are to form on the right of the standard and which on the left.

6. The Regulations About Military Crimes
to Be Given to the Troops

When the troops have been organized and the squads formed, the
tagma should assemble by dekarchies. It is well if the men are already
familiar with the regulations about military crimes set down in the

17

laws. Otherwise a written copy should be given to the commanding officer so he can explain them to the men when they have more time.[15]

(1) If a soldier disobeys his own pentarch or tetrarch, he shall be punished. And if a pentarch or tetrarch disobeys his dekarch, or dekarch his hekatontarch, they shall likewise be punished.

(2) If any member of the tagma shall dare to do this to his commanding officer, the count or the tribune of the tagma, he shall undergo capital punishment.

(3) If a soldier is unjustly treated by anyone, he shall appeal to the commanding officer of his tagma, but if unjustly treated by that commanding officer himself, he shall go to the next-higher officer.

(4) If anyone presumes to stay beyond the time of his furlough, he shall be dismissed from the army and as a civilian handed over to the civil authorities.

(5) If any soldiers dare, for any reason whatsoever, to enter into a conspiracy, sedition, or mutiny against their commanding officer, they shall undergo capital punishment, in particular the ringleaders of any such conspiracy or mutiny.

(6) If anyone who has been entrusted with the defense of a city or fortress shall betray the same or shall desert his post against the orders of his commanding officer, he shall undergo the extreme penalty.

(7) If anyone be found guilty of wanting to desert to the enemy, he shall undergo the extreme penalty, not only he but also anyone who knew of it, because he knew yet did not report it to the commanding officer.

(8) If anyone after hearing the orders of his dekarch does not carry them out, he shall be punished. But if he does not do so out of ignorance of the orders, the dekarch should be punished for not having informed him beforehand.

(9) If anyone finds a stray animal or any other object, small or large, and does not report it and turn it over to his commanding officer, he shall be punished, not only he but anyone who knows about it, as thieves both of them.

(10) If anyone causes injury to a taxpayer and refuses to make compensation, he shall repay double the amount of the damage.

(11) If anyone who receives an allowance for the purpose

15. The regulations have been numbered consecutively in Chapters 6, 7, 8.

neglects his own weapons,[16] and if his dekarch shall not force him to acquire them or not report him to the commanding officer, then both the soldier himself and the dekarch shall be punished.

7. The Regulations About Military Crimes to Be Given to the Tagmatic Commanders

(12) Anyone who disobeys his own commanding officer shall be punished according to the laws.

(13) Anyone who injures a soldier shall compensate him by paying back twice the amount; and he shall pay a like sum if he causes injury to a taxpayer. If, in winter quarters, or in camp, or on the march, either an officer or a soldier shall cause injury to a taxpayer without making proper restitution, he shall pay him back twice the amount.

(14) If in time of war anyone should presume to let a soldier go off on furlough, he shall pay a fine of thirty nomismata. While in winter quarters, furloughs may be allowed for two or three months, and in time of peace, the soldier may be allowed to go on furlough within the boundaries of the province.

(15) If anyone who is entrusted with the defense of the city or a fortress should surrender it or evacuate it while still able to defend it, unless compelled by danger to life, he shall undergo capital punishment.

After these regulations on crimes have been read, the tagmas should be drawn up in battle formation, and the punishments for offenses during combat made known to the assembled troops.

8. Military Punishments

After the organization of the tagmas, the following list of punishments should be read out in Latin and in Greek.

(16) If during the time when the battle lines are being formed and during combat a soldier shall abandon his post or his standard and flee, or if he charges out ahead of the place where he has been stationed, or if he plunders the dead, or races off to pursue the

16. The text has *reparationa*, deriving from the Latin *reparatio*. Leo VI (*Tactical Constitutions*, 8, 11) understands this in its usual sense of time for restoration, i.e., vacation. The Ambrosian paraphrase of the *Strategikon* (fol. 126') equates it with *philotimia*, a gratuity or allowance.

enemy, or attacks the baggage train or camp of the enemy, we order that he be executed, and that all the loot he may have taken be confiscated and given in to the common fund of his tagma, inasmuch as he has broken ranks and has betrayed his comrades.

(17) If during a general action or battle the troops who had formed for combat should turn back—may this never happen—without a good and manifest cause, we order that the soldiers of the tagma which first took to flight and turned back from the line of battle or from their own meros be shot down and decimated by the other tagmas, inasmuch as they broke their ranks and were to blame for the rout of the entire meros. But if it should happen that some of them were wounded in the battle itself, they shall be exempt from such a judgment.

(18) If a standard should be captured by the enemy—may this never happen—without a good and manifest excuse, we order that those charged with guarding the banner be punished and reduced to the lowest rank in their unit or the schola in which they are registered. If it happens that any were wounded in the fighting, they shall be exempt from such punishment.

(19) If a meros or the whole formation is routed—may this never happen—when a camp is nearby, and if the men do not retire toward the defenders or seek refuge within the camp itself, but carelessly run off in some other direction, we order that those daring to do this be punished for disregarding their comrades.

(20) If a soldier throws away his arms in battle, we order that he be punished for disarming himself and arming the enemy.

9. The Orderly Way of Marching Through Our Own Country When There Is No Hostile Activity

A large army should not be assembled in one place when there is no hostile activity, for with time on their hands the soldiers may give themselves to sedition and improper plans.

When battle is expected the army must march in formation, proceeding either by moira or by meros. For marching in formation is much safer for the soldiers both in our own and in hostile territory. It is very important that each moira accustom its own baggage train to follow behind with its own standards, as described elsewhere, and not become mixed up with that of another unit. While the enemy is at a distance the march should be by moira or meros. The whole army should not be brought together in one place because the men might quickly find themselves starving, the army's size could be easily estimated by the enemy, and fodder might be hard to obtain. As they are drawing closer to the enemy, about six, seven, or even ten days away, the troops should be drawn in closer together and at the same time set up camp, as is explained in the section on camps.

If the march is in unknown regions or places, surveyors should go out a day in advance with the duty of surveying the entire location in which camp is to be made, and to apportion a certain section equitably to each meros. The quartering parties should also ride a day ahead to reconnoiter for water and forage.

When the troops on campaign encounter very rough, steep, heavily wooded, or other difficult terrain, some soldiers should be sent ahead to clear and level the land as much as possible, so that the horses may not be worn out. The men detailed for this should not belong to a scouting troop or other special unit.

When the army is on the march, the commanding general should be at its head with his own specially chosen troops preceding him as an honor guard. With them should be their spare horses and the bucellary standards. Directly behind him should come the spatharioi, then the bucellary troops, and finally their supply train.[17] The commanding officer of each meros or moira should arrange his own column in like manner, whether marching as part of a larger command or alone.

At river crossings or other difficult places in unknown country, quartering parties should go ahead and, after first investigating the area, should inform the general what the country is like, and competent officers should make dispositions to cover the passage. If the places are unusually difficult, then the commanding general himself should leave the column and remain at the place until everyone has safely crossed over. But the general should do this only if the enemy is not in the vicinity. For in that case he must not stay about, but the commanding officer of each meros should perform that duty until all of his command is safely past. Otherwise everyone will try to get ahead at once, which would only cause friction and injury.

Cultivated fields must be spared, and troops should not march through them, and they should cause no damage to taxpayers. But if it is absolutely necessary to pass through the fields, orders should be

17. Spatharios: sword bearer, apparently an aide.

given for the commanding officer of each moira or meros to remain until the tagmas under his command have passed through. He should turn over the fields in good condition to the next unit and then leave the area. In turn each commanding officer after him is to perform the same duty, and in this way the good order of the general and the security of the farmer will be maintained.

If, when the going is expected to be difficult, wild animals are startled or encountered along the road, chasing them is to be forbidden, for this causes noise and confusion and wears out the horses to no purpose. In time of peace, however, hunting is necessary for the soldiers.

If the army is small, an effort should be made not to have it march through inhabited areas, whether friendly or hostile, so that it might not be observed by spies and the information relayed to the enemy, but it should advance by other routes.

· B O O K I I ·
The Cavalry Battle Formation

1. The Utility and Necessity of Forming the Army in Two Lines

To form the whole army simply in one line facing the enemy for a general cavalry battle and to hold nothing in reserve for various eventualities in case of a reverse is the mark of an inexperienced and absolutely reckless man. For it is not, as some laymen might imagine, by the number of bodies, by unquestioning boldness, or by plain assault that battles are decided but, under God, by strategy and skill. Strategy makes use of times and places, surprises and various tricks to outwit the enemy with the idea of achieving its objectives even without actual fighting. Strategy is essential to survival and is the true characteristic of an intelligent and courageous general. Skill enables the army to maintain discipline and coordination, as well as its own safety, while varying its battle formations and attacks, and not only to foil the wiles of the enemy but to turn them against them. With this in mind the older military writers organized their armies into droungoi, divisions, and moiras of varying strength as conditions dictated, just as the Avars and Turks line up today keeping themselves in that formation, and so they can be quickly called to support any unit that may give way in battle. For they do not draw themselves up in one battle line only, as do the Romans and Persians, staking the fate of tens of thousands of horsemen on a single throw. But they form two, sometimes even three lines, distributing the units in depth, especially when their troops are numerous, and they can easily undertake any sort of action. To draw up the whole army in one battle line, especially if it is composed of lancers, is, in our opinion, to invite a host of evils. If it is a large army, it will have to stretch over a great distance; part of it will be located on unfavorable terrain, the length of the line will cause it to be disordered and hard to manage, there will be no coordination between the units, and as a result, it may well break up even before contact with the enemy. Then, if it should be outflanked or unexpectedly attacked by the enemy, and it has no support from its rear or its flanks, without any protection or reserve force, it will be forced to retire in headlong flight.

Furthermore, in actual combat nobody can properly supervise the entire battle, since the line is spread out so far, and some can desert from their bandons unnoticed, and give all the others an excuse to retreat. If they do retreat, there is no way of turning back or of checking the flight, for nobody is able to get them back since, as we said, the whole army is routed. Sometimes troops formed in a single line may seem to be winning the battle and driving the enemy back, but in the melee their formation will certainly have become broken up and the pursuit will be disorderly. If the fleeing enemy should turn upon the pursuers as the Scythians frequently do, or if some other force should suddenly appear out of ambush, then the pursuers will certainly be forced to take to flight since, as mentioned above, there is nobody to ward off this unexpected attack. It seems that forming all the troops in a single line has one advantage, actually an advantage in appearance only, that is, at a distance such a line will appear very large and imposing and can readily be employed in encircling movements, but this can also be accomplished easily in other ways which will be explained later. We believe that, as far as human reasoning goes, there are many exceptionally compelling reasons which lead to the conclusion that there should be two lines, one of them a support, according to the diagram given below. First, the troops in the front line will fight more eagerly knowing that their rear is protected by the second line, and their flanks by the flank guards. Second, a man in the first line is not as likely to run away when he knows that many other soldiers are stationed to his rear, that is in the second line, and will see anyone deserting his post. In combat this can be extremely important. Supposing that the first line retreats or is pushed back, then the second line is there as a support and a place of refuge. This makes it possible to rally the troops and get them to turn back against their attackers. Also when we are pursuing the enemy, we can make our attack safely, for if some of the enemy turn back on us or if there is a sudden attack from another quarter, then the second line can hold its ground, join battle, and protect the first. In addition, if the first line is actually routed, so that it cannot be brought back into action against the enemy, the second line, still in good order, will easily join battle with the enemy, even though, as mentioned, they have routed the first line. For the enemy's formation will necessarily be broken up and disordered by the fighting when it meets a force still in good order, such as the second line. The most compelling reason of all is that not only is the double line of battle, as said, appropriate against an enemy force equal in numbers, but also against superior forces, which is clear from reason and from a study of the diagram below.

Perhaps some may object that if the first line is thrown into confusion or driven back, the second will also easily be pushed back with it. Our answer is that if victory seems precarious with two lines, what hope can there be when there is only one line and that one breaks up? To the further objection that the army's formation is weakened by dividing it into two battle lines, we would admit this to be valid if the force were really divided and half of it kept out of action. But as a matter of fact, we have not divided the force, we have merely changed its formation. What happened is that the entire force which was previously deployed in a long and thin straight line, we have now formed in two lines. We have taken none of it out of action, but have only modified its disposition and by the methods described increased its strength.

2. Arrangement of the Tagmas in the Line of Battle

For the above reasons, every cavalry army, whether large or of average strength, must be divided into moiras and divisions, or the so-called droungoi, of varying size. Obviously the general must use all the resources of his intelligence to avoid, as best he can, openly engaging in battle an army greatly outnumbering his own, especially if he is fighting against nations that carry on warfare in an organized fashion. If an army composed of infantry is present, it should be formed as explained in the book on that subject. If the whole force is mounted, and it is to fight against other mounted troops, divide the cavalry into three lines. Form the first line, called the promachos, into three equal divisions, each division or meros composed of three moiras. The lieutenant general should take his post in the center meros, the other two merarchs in the divisions on either side, each in the center between the moirarchs under his command.

3. Assault Troops and Defenders

The proportion of assault troops and of defenders in these divisions should be such that a third of each meros consists of assault troops, preferably archers, stationed on the flanks; the remaining two thirds, in the center of each meros, should consist of defenders.

4. Flank Guards and Outflankers

To the side of the left meros of this first line where hostile outflanking and encircling movements may naturally be expected, station two or three bandons as flank guards, their front aligned with that of the meros. To the side of the right meros station a bandon or two of archers, known as outflankers. Form the second line, referred to as the support, and which should consist of about a third of the whole army, into four divisions, as shown in the diagram below, stationed at a bowshot's distance from one another's flanks. Make these divisions double-fronted in order to meet attacks from the rear. From the two end divisions of this line a bandon or two should be dropped about a bowshot behind on both sides to form a third line, the rear guard. To make those convenient intervals between the divisions of the second line aligned all the way and to make the entire second line appear to be one body of troops and not be thrown into disorder when moving about, one or more bandons must be stationed in these intervals along the entire distance of the clear space. They should be two or more cavalrymen deep or, better, four or more, depending on the size of the army. As a result, when it is time to provide refuge for the retreating units of the first line, these three bandons drawn up in the clear spaces are withdrawn back to the rear guard, leaving the clear spaces free for the retiring troops. In this way they make the clear spaces into a refuge for the troops being driven back, as we have shown, and at the same time they can turn back men trying to desert further to the rear. Moreover, when they form in the third line with the rear guard, they can aid in repulsing any enemy forces appearing in the rear to harass the second line and so keep that sector intact. Now, if the army is of medium strength, that is, from five to ten or twelve thousand, the second line should consist of two divisions instead of four, leaving one clear space to receive the retreating troops. If the army contains less than five thousand, the second line should consist of only one division.

26

5. Ambushes to the Rear or the Flanks of the Enemy's Line

In addition to the above, three or four bandons, called ambush troops, should be detailed to both sides of the battle line, in the manner explained elsewhere. They are to prevent the enemy from trying to ambush our left, and they can themselves lay ambushes against the enemy's right if the terrain is favorable. It should be noted that well-timed attacks against the enemy's flanks and rear are much more effective and decisive than direct frontal charges and attacks. If the enemy force is smaller, such attacks catching them by surprise inflict greater damage, since the troops driven back will find it difficult to reach safety. If the enemy force is equal to ours or even superior, it will find itself in a serious struggle, believing that the attacking troops are numerous. Consequently, a small army should not prepare to face an organized and more numerous foe in open battle except in case of necessity. If the necessity does arise, do not mass all your troops in front, and even if the enemy is superior in numbers, direct your operations against his rear or his flanks. For it is dangerous and uncertain under all conditions and against any people to engage in purely frontal combat, even if the enemy stations a smaller number of troops up front.

To sum up, all the cavalry tagmas are divided into a first and a second line, in the manner described, especially if the army is large. They are detailed as defenders, as assault troops, as flank guards, as outflankers, as ambush troops, as support troops, as rear guard.

6. Depth of Formation

As far as the depth of the line is concerned, the ancient authorities wrote that it had formerly been regarded as sufficient to form the ranks four deep in each tagma, greater depth being viewed as useless and serving no purpose. For there can be no pressure from the rear up through the ranks, as happens with an infantry formation, which may force the men in front to push forward against their will. Horses cannot use their heads to push people in front of them evenly, as can infantry. The file leaders, those stationed in front, receive no assistance from additional ranks, whether lancers or archers. The lances of the ranks behind the fourth cannot reach beyond the front; the archers are forced to shoot up high because of all the men in front of them, and the result is that their arrows are ineffectual in

27

battle against the enemy. Anyone doubting this will be convinced by actual experience. As stated, therefore, a depth of four ranks used to be enough.

Since, however, it is true that the number of outstanding soldiers, those capable of acting as file leaders in hand-to-hand combat, in any tagma is limited, it is necessary to regulate the depth of formation according to the type of unit. So it is that the Federati, drawn up in the center of the first line, are formed to a depth of seven men, followed by a serving boy if enough can be found; and their dekarchies should be organized accordingly. The companies of the Vexillations to their left should also have dekarchies of about seven men; the Illyrikians on the right should have dekarchies of about eight men.[1] The other tagmas made up of ordinary troops should be organized with eight or ten men to a dekarchy. If it happens that some of these more ordinary tagmas are stationed in the first line, then put eight or ten men in each file, since these tagmas are weaker. The tagmas of the Optimates, however, since they are picked troops and are usually stationed in the second line, should have about five regular soldiers followed by two men at arms, so that the dekarchy should have seven men. These depths we have prescribed should remain the same in the event that these tagmas should be moved up to the first line. Foreign contingents, if stationed by themselves, should be drawn up according to their own customs. It is advantageous to employ them as assault and ambush troops.

The depth, therefore, must be no more than eight or at most ten men, no matter how weak the tagmas might be, nor should it be less than five, even for the best units, for the depths made in the above manner and in the proper proportions are adequate. The length of the first battle line, that is, the number of front rank men, should not be greatly reduced. The injudicious practice up to the present has been to form all the tagmas equally ten deep, with the result that

1. Vexillation in the third century designated first an infantry, then a cavalry detachment. The term came to be applied, as here, to a regular army division, but not much is known about its evolution.

    The Illyrikians, *equites Illyriciani*, formed part of the local defense forces in the provinces of Phoenicia, Syria, Palestine, Osrhoene, Mesopotamia, and Arabia: see John Wiita, "The Ethnika in Byzantine Military Treatises" (Ph.D. diss., University of Minnesota, 1977), 22. In the 630s we find a soldier of the fifteenth bandon of the Illyrikians in winter quarters near Caesarea in Palestine: *Acta S. Anastasii Persae*, ed. H. Usener, Programma Universitatis Bonnae (1884), 26.

when they are lined up for inspection spies can easily and quickly
estimate the strength of the whole army by counting the file leaders,
assuming that this is the regulation depth and about the same proportion is maintained. The second line is composed of the remaining
men. It is clear, as explained above, that the men at arms are drawn
up with the tagmas of the Optimates, and with the Federati those
serving boys fit for such service.

7. Squads

Squads should be made up of old and young men in proper proportion. Otherwise the older men, if formed by themselves, may
be weak, and the younger, inexperienced men may turn out
disorganized.

8. Armament

Armament should vary as follows. In the first line the file leader and
the man behind him, the second in the file, and the last man should
all bear lances. All the others, drawn up in the middle, who know
how to shoot, should be archers, and without shields. For it is impossible to draw the bow effectively on horseback while also carrying a
shield on the left arm.

9. Medical Corpsmen

In addition to the above, eight or ten of the less-skilled soldiers in
each tagma should be assigned as medical corpsmen to each bandon,
especially in the first battle line. They should be alert, quick, lightly
clothed, and without weapons. Their duty is to follow about a hundred feet to the rear of their own tagma,[2] to pick up and give aid to
anyone seriously wounded in the battle, or who has fallen off his
horse, or is otherwise out of action, so they may not be trampled by
the second line or die through neglect of their wounds. For each
person so rescued the corpsman should receive from the treasury
one nomisma over and above his pay. Then when the second line has
passed and driven back the enemy, they should collect the spoils

2. The Roman foot, which may still have been in use, was equal to 29.6
   centimeters, whereas the standard Byzantine foot came to 31.23 cm.:
   E. Schilbach, *Byzantinische Metrologie* (Munich 1970), 13–16.

29

from the enemy dead left on the field of the first battle, and hand them over to the dekarchs or file leaders of their own tagma, receiving a share of it back from the dekarchs as a reward for their work. For we regard letting them have this as an equitable and suitable perquisite for the file leaders when they are victorious in combat, since more than any others they have to do most of the fighting in the first onslaught, and also they cannot be allowed the chance to dismount and break ranks to collect plunder themselves.

To make it easier for the corpsmen and the wounded or fallen to mount the rescue horses, they should place both stirrups on the left side of the saddle, one to the front, as is customary, the other behind it. When two want to get up on the horse, the corpsman and the man who is out of action, the first mounts by the regular stirrup to the front, the other by the one to the back. It is also essential that they carry flasks of water for men who may be fainting from their wounds.

10. Lance Pennons

We do not recommend carrying pennons on the lances during battle. For they are as useless in combat as they are valuable for presenting a fine appearance at inspections, sieges, or parades. For whether throwing or stabbing with the lance, the pennon reduces both accuracy and range, and when the shooting begins, it interferes with the fire of the archers in the rear ranks. Moreover, in charging, in retreating, in wheeling about, it is no slight inconvenience, and for this reason it should not be used in combat. It is possible, however, to keep both, the fine appearance of the battle line at a distance as well as utility. The pennons may be flown until the enemy is about a mile away, then they should be furled and put back into their cases.

11. Spies or Scouts

In addition, spies or scouts should be assigned to each tagma of the Optimates and Federati, and to each meros of the ordinary troops, two to a tagma, eight or twelve to a meros. They should be sober, alert, healthy, and good looking. Stationed at intervals, depending on the nature of the terrain, before the battle and until it is all over, they should keep both the enemy and their own units under observation to prevent any attack from ambush or any other hostile trick.

12. Surveyors and Quartering Parties

In addition, there should also be a like number of surveyors who should, along with the quartering parties, go ahead and lay out the camp site. The same number of quartering or preparation troops should be detailed with them to go ahead, reconnoiter the roads, and guide the army to the camp.

13. Distances Between Units and Battle Lines

When the battle line is formed as described above and illustrated in the diagram, it is necessary for the divisions of the first line to move about close enough to one another, so that the distance or interval between one meros and another is not great, but enough to keep them from crowding each other while marching and to make them appear clearly separated. The flank guards should march close in until near the enemy; then they should move out to the side about a bowshot from the left meros, no more, especially if the enemy line is longer than ours.[3] The outflankers should be in a similar position on the right, as the situation may require. The divisions of the second line should be about a bowshot from one another's side. Until the enemy is nearby, this line should follow the first at a distance of a mile or more,[4] depending on the terrain, so that, as far as possible, it follows along unseen to keep the enemy from observing it from a distance and changing their tactics accordingly. But when the enemy get close and see the second line, they have no time left to change their plans; then the second line should move up about four bow-shots from the first and regulate its moves in accord with it. For during battle it should not be so far behind the first line that it cannot provide support, nor should it be so close that it may get mixed up with it in battle, especially when a lot of dust is being kicked up. If

3. A bowshot (flight range, not accurate target range) was about 300 meters: W. McLeod, "The Range of the Ancient Bow," *Phoenix: The Journal of the Classical Association of Canada* 19 (1965): 1–14. Schilbach (*Byzantinische Metrologie*, 42) puts it at 328.84 meters. A. Bivar, however ("Cavalry Equipment and Tactics on the Euphrates Frontier," *Dumbarton Oaks Papers* 26 [1972]: 283), measures a bowshot in the *Strategikon* as about 133 meters.
4. The Roman mile, probably still standard in the time of Maurice, was 1,480 meters: Schilbach, *Byzantinische Metrologie*, 32–36. But in Book IX Maurice assumes that there are 5,000 or 5,155 Byzantine feet, which should be 31.23 cm. each, to a mile.

too close, this second line may attack before the enemy's ranks are broken up in pursuit of the first line, which will still be in disarray and unable to cooperate with it. The tagmas stationed on both sides to the rear of the flanks of the second line should be about a bowshot behind to guard its rear and should follow at the same distance.

14. The Size and Variety of Flags

In each meros the flags or standards of the tagmas should be fairly small and easy to carry. We cannot account for their having become so large and cumbersome. The only distinctive feature should be in their streamers. But the flags of the moirarchs should be larger and of different design. In like manner, those of the merarchs should differ from the moirarchs under their command. The flag of the lieutenant general should differ from those of the merarchs. Finally, that of the general should be clearly distinctive, more conspicuous than all the others, and familiar to all, so that in case of a reverse the troops, seeing it, may easily, as has been said, rally and regroup.

15. The Color Guard

When all the flags have been set up along the length of the line as shown in the diagram, fifteen or even twenty of the best men of the unit should be detailed to guard and defend each flag.

16. The Posts of Officers

Superior officers should be stationed in safe places, so they do not dash forward and fall in battle, which would discourage the soldiers. For if one of the subordinate officers should fall, nobody will find out about it except the men of his own tagma. But if one of the more prominent officers falls, his death, as it becomes known to all or most of the troops, causes faintheartedness through the whole army. Therefore, when the army is one or two bowshots from the enemy's battle line, the lieutenant general and the merarchs should station themselves on the same line as the standards and there supervise and regulate the formation. When the charge is just about to begin, their best men, who are stationed on either side of them, should move in front of them as a screen, and they are the ones who should engage in close combat. The general himself, up to the moment of the charge, is to direct the formation, supervise, and adapt to the movements of the enemy. At that moment he should join his own tagma which is drawn up, not for battle, but as a sort of landmark and guide for the first and second lines, that is, in the middle of the second line.

17. Trumpets

We do not consider it desirable that many trumpets be sounded or blown during battle, for this causes disturbance and confusion, and commands cannc. be properly understood. If the ground is level, then one trumpet is enough, and it should be sounded in the center meros in each battle line. If the ground is uneven, or if a violent wind or the noise of water makes it difficult to hear the orders clearly, then it may be well to blow one trumpet in each of the other divisions, so that three will be sounded in the whole battle line. The better silence is observed, the less disturbed will the younger men be and the less excited the horses, and the more fearsome will the battle line appear to the enemy, and it will be easy to recognize the commands. For these reasons, any sound at all is out of place after the line has begun to move into action.

18. The Battle Cry Sometimes Used

The battle cry, "Nobiscum," which it was customary to shout when beginning the charge is, in our opinion, extremely dangerous and harmful. Shouting it at that moment may cause the ranks to break up. For because of the shout, the more timid soldiers in approaching really close combat may hesitate before the clash, while the bolder, roused to anger, may rashly push forward and break ranks. The same problem occurs with the horses, for they too differ in temperament. The result is that the battle line is uneven and without cohesion, in fact, its ranks may well be broken even before the charge, which is very dangerous.

Instead of the shout, prayers should be said in camp on the actual day of battle before anyone goes out the gate. All, led by the priests, the general, and the other officers, should recite the "Kyrie eleison" (Lord have mercy) for some time in unison. Then, in hopes of success, each meros should shout the "Nobiscum Deus" (God is with

33

us) three times as it marches out of camp.[5] As soon as the army leaves the camp to form for battle, absolute silence should prevail, and no unnecessary word should be spoken. For this keeps the army in better order, and the commands of the officers are more readily understood. The full spirit of the charge is conveyed by the very circumstances, the necessary closing of ranks, and the presence of the enemy, and no other sign is needed. But when the army closes with the enemy, it is not a bad idea for the men to shout and cheer, especially the rear ranks, to unnerve the enemy and stir up our own troops.

19. Heralds

The function of the heralds, it seems to us, is a useful one, inasmuch as before the battle they address the troops to encourage them and get them to recall their previous victories. When their speech is finished, each tagma should be formed and drilled.

20. The Use of Two Standards

Since we know that the enemy generally bases his estimates of the strength of an army on the number of standards, we think it necessary for each tagma to have two standards, both the same. One is the regular standard, in the name of the count or tribune of each tagma. The other is that of the hekatontarch, who is also called the ilarch. Both should be carried by the tagma and held in equal honor until the day of battle. On the day of battle only the one regular standard should be raised, for flying a large number of banners causes confusion and the men may not recognize their own. In this way it is possible for the army to appear strong by the number of standards, and still on the day of battle have the regular one easily recognized. Tagmas which are greatly reduced in strength should not be allowed to fly their standards in open battle, but should take their stand under another one, the reason being that because they are few in number they will not be able to protect their own, and having many banners flying would cause confusion in the meros. As stated, however, arrange matters so that each bandon has no less than two hundred men and no more than four hundred.

5. The same invocation is found in Vegetius, *Ep. rei milit.*, 3, 5.

·BOOK III·
Formations of the Tagma

1. The Symbols Used to Illustrate the Formations of the Tagma

✝   The Standard

X   Commanding Officer of the Tagma

b   Trumpeter

k̃   Cape bearer

þ̣   Hekatontarch or Ilarch

ſ   Dekarch with lance and shield

k̬   Pentarch with lance and shield

k̆   Third in file, with bow but no shield

k̥   Fourth in file, rear guard with bow and shield

k̩   Fifth in file, with bow but no shield

K   Cavalryman or soldier with whatever weapon he can handle

2. Formation of the Tagma Assuming a Strength of 310 Men

This is the plan of the tagma when it has been drawn up for battle and begins its advance. It should definitely march in open order so that the cavalrymen will not be crowded together and become fatigued before the fighting. They should be far enough apart for each one to turn his horse about easily when he wishes. The command for this is: "Open order. March."[1] Then, riding at ease, the soldiers advance against the enemy, as illustrated in the diagram.[2]

1. *Largiter ambula.*
2. In the Laurentian manuscript only the central body of troops is indicated.

35

Þ í í í í í í í í
ʀ̌ ʀ̌ ʀ̌ ʀ̌ ʀ̌ ʀ̌ ʀ̌ ʀ̌ ʀ̌
ʞ̌ ʞ̌ ʞ̌ ʞ̌ ʞ̌ ʞ̌ ʞ̌ ʞ̌ ʞ̌
ʀ̌ ʀ̌ ʀ̌ ʀ̌ ʀ̌ ʀ̌ ʀ̌ ʀ̌ ʀ̌
K K K K K K K K K K
K K K K K K K K K K
K K K K K K K K K K
K K K K K K K K K K
K K K K K K K K K K
ʀ̌ ʀ̌ ʀ̌ ʀ̌ ʀ̌ ʀ̌ ʀ̌ ʀ̌ ʀ̌

í í í í x ✝ í í í í í
ʀ̌ ʀ̌ ʀ̌ ʀ̌ b ʀ̌ ʀ̌ ʀ̌ ʀ̌ ʀ̌
ʞ̌ ʞ̌ ʞ̌ ʞ̌ ʞ̌ ʞ̌ ʞ̌ ʞ̌ ʞ̌ ʞ̌
ʀ̌ ʀ̌ ʀ̌ ʀ̌ ʀ̌ ʀ̌ ʀ̌ ʀ̌ ʀ̌ ʀ̌
K K K K K K K K K K K
K K K K K K K K K K K
K K K K K K K K K K K
K K K K K K K K K K K
K K K K K K K K K K K
ʀ̌ ʀ̌ ʀ̌ ʀ̌ ʀ̌ ʀ̌ ʀ̌ ʀ̌ ʀ̌ ʀ̌

í í í í í í í í í Þ
ʀ̌ ʀ̌ ʀ̌ ʀ̌ ʀ̌ ʀ̌ ʀ̌ ʀ̌ ʀ̌
ʞ̌ ʞ̌ ʞ̌ ʞ̌ ʞ̌ ʞ̌ ʞ̌ ʞ̌ ʞ̌
ʀ̌ ʀ̌ ʀ̌ ʀ̌ ʀ̌ ʀ̌ ʀ̌ ʀ̌ ʀ̌
K K K K K K K K K K
K K K K K K K K K K
K K K K K K K K K K
K K K K K K K K K K
K K K K K K K K K K
ʀ̌ ʀ̌ ʀ̌ ʀ̌ ʀ̌ ʀ̌ ʀ̌ ʀ̌ ʀ̌

3. Plan of the Same Tagma with Its Flanks in Close Order

When, with the enemy about a mile away, the decision is made to close up on the flank, the command is: "By the Flank. Close." [3] The files of cavalrymen move up closer to each other continuing their advance toward the enemy, as is shown in the diagram.

Þ í í í í í í í í
ʀ̌ ʀ̌ ʀ̌ ʀ̌ ʀ̌ ʀ̌ ʀ̌ ʀ̌ ʀ̌
ʞ̌ ʞ̌ ʞ̌ ʞ̌ ʞ̌ ʞ̌ ʞ̌ ʞ̌ ʞ̌
ʀ̌ ʀ̌ ʀ̌ ʀ̌ ʀ̌ ʀ̌ ʀ̌ ʀ̌ ʀ̌
K K K K K K K K K K
K K K K K K K K K K
K K K K K K K K K K
K K K K K K K K K K
K K K K K K K K K K
ʀ̌ ʀ̌ ʀ̌ ʀ̌ ʀ̌ ʀ̌ ʀ̌ ʀ̌ ʀ̌

í í í x ✝ í í í í í
ʀ̌ ʀ̌ ʀ̌ b ʀ̌ ʀ̌ ʀ̌ ʀ̌ ʀ̌ ʀ̌
ʞ̌ ʞ̌ ʞ̌ ʞ̌ ʞ̌ ʞ̌ ʞ̌ ʞ̌ ʞ̌ ʞ̌
ʀ̌ ʀ̌ ʀ̌ ʀ̌ ʀ̌ ʀ̌ ʀ̌ ʀ̌ ʀ̌ ʀ̌
K K K K K K K K K K K
K K K K K K K K K K K
K K K K K K K K K K K
K K K K K K K K K K K
K K K K K K K K K K K
ʀ̌ ʀ̌ ʀ̌ ʀ̌ ʀ̌ ʀ̌ ʀ̌ ʀ̌ ʀ̌ ʀ̌

í í í í í í í í í Þ
ʀ̌ ʀ̌ ʀ̌ ʀ̌ ʀ̌ ʀ̌ ʀ̌ ʀ̌ ʀ̌
ʞ̌ ʞ̌ ʞ̌ ʞ̌ ʞ̌ ʞ̌ ʞ̌ ʞ̌ ʞ̌
ʀ̌ ʀ̌ ʀ̌ ʀ̌ ʀ̌ ʀ̌ ʀ̌ ʀ̌ ʀ̌
K K K K K K K K K K
K K K K K K K K K K
K K K K K K K K K K
K K K K K K K K K K
K K K K K K K K K K
ʀ̌ ʀ̌ ʀ̌ ʀ̌ ʀ̌ ʀ̌ ʀ̌ ʀ̌ ʀ̌

The diagram has been expanded to make it reach a strength of 310 men, as required by the text. For variations in the diagrams in the other manuscripts, see G. Dennis, ed., *Das Strategikon des Maurikios*, Corpus fontium historiae byzantinae, 17 (Vienna, 1981): 502–509.

3. *Ad latus stringe.*

4. Plan of the Same Tagma with Both Flanks and Rear in Close Order

When, within three or four bowshots of the enemy line, the decision is made to close up by the flanks and by the rear, depending on the circumstances, the command is: "Close ranks."[4] They then gradually close up while continuing the advance. The archers open fire, and the whole line together in close order begins the charge, as the diagram shows.

Ᵽ Í Í Í Í Í Í Í Í   Í Í Í   X   †   Í Í Í Í Í Í   Í Í Í Í Í Í Í Í Ᵽ
Ř Ř Ř Ř Ř Ř Ř Ř Ř   Ř Ř Ř   b   Ř   Ř Ř Ř Ř Ř   Ř Ř Ř Ř Ř Ř Ř Ř Ř
Ř Ř Ř Ř Ř Ř Ř Ř Ř   Ř Ř Ř   Ř   Ř   Ř Ř Ř Ř Ř   Ř Ř Ř Ř Ř Ř Ř Ř Ř
Ř Ř Ř Ř Ř Ř Ř Ř Ř   Ř Ř Ř   Ř   Ř   Ř Ř Ř Ř Ř   Ř Ř Ř Ř Ř Ř Ř Ř Ř
K K K K K K K K K   K K K   K   K   K K K K K K   K K K K K K K K K
K K K K K K K K K   K K K   K   K   K K K K K K   K K K K K K K K K
K K K K K K K K K   K K K   K   K   K K K K K K   K K K K K K K K K
K K K K K K K K K   K K K   K   K   K K K K K K   K K K K K K K K K
K K K K K K K K K   K K K   K   K   K K K K K K   K K K K K K K K K
Ř Ř Ř Ř Ř Ř Ř Ř Ř   Ř Ř Ř   Ř   Ř   Ř Ř Ř Ř Ř   Ř Ř Ř Ř Ř Ř Ř Ř Ř

5. Method of Drilling the Tagma

When the bandon has been drawn up in proper order, the herald shouts the following commands. "Silence. Do not fall back. Do not go ahead of the standard. Advance even with the front rank. Keep your eyes on the standard. Follow it with your company, soldier. This is how a brave soldier should act. If you leave the standard, you will not be victorious. Soldier, keep to your assigned position. Standard bearer, keep to your position. Whether fighting, or pursuing the enemy, or in the front ranks, do not charge out impetuously and cause your ranks to be broken up."[5]

4. Junge.
5. Silentium. nemo demittat, nemo antecedat bandum. sic venias vero aequalis facies. bandum capta, ipso seque cum bando milix. talis est comodum miles barbati. si vero bandum demittes eo modo non vero vices. serva milix ordinem positum. ipsum serve et

A single tagma should be drilled as follows. At a given signal, advance and halt either while at attention or on the run. If the commander wants the troops to advance, he shouts out: "March,"[6] which would be *kineson* in Greek. This signal may also be given by bugle or by motion of the lance pennon. And so the tagma advances. If he wants it to stop, he shouts the command: "Halt,"[7] or he gives the signal by banging a shield, by a hand motion, or by trumpet. And so the tagma halts.

In case he first wants them to march in open order, the command is: "In line. March."[8] To close ranks with the greatest precision by the flanks and the rear, as illustrated in the above diagrams, the command is: "By the flank. Close"; the dekarchs: "To the dekarchs"; the pentarchs: "To the pentarchs."[9] Then all the troops, side by side, close in on each other, not to one flank, but from both sides closing upon the center, that is, upon the standard bearer. This maneuver should also be practiced by the meros, for in this fashion ranks may be closed quickly and in good order. Just as the dekarchs align themselves, so the tetrarchs or fileclosers should align themselves. For if they close ranks accurately, they effectively keep the troops in front of them from abandoning their posts in combat and fleeing to the rear.

At the command, "Close ranks,"[10] the soldiers close up from the rear for the charge. With the troops marching in close formation, particularly after they have closed in tightly from the flank, the archers open fire, and the command is given: "Charge."[11] The dekarchs and pentarchs then lean forward, cover their heads and part of their horses' necks with their shields, hold their lances high as their shoulders in the manner of the fair-haired races, and protected by their shields they ride on in good order, not too fast but at a trot, to avoid having the impetus of their charge break up their ranks before coming to blows with the enemy, which is a real risk. All the archers to the rear should open fire.

---

tu *bandifer. sive pugnas sive seques inimicum sive aequalis facies, non forte minare ut ne sparges tu suum ordinem.*

6. *Move.*
7. *Sta.*
8. *Equaliter ambula.*
9. *Ad latus stringe. ad decarchas. ad pentarchas.*
10. *Junge.*
11. *Percute.*

In pursuing the enemy, they should sometimes charge in open order, sometimes together in close order. If in open order, the command is: "Charge at a gallop." [12] And they should ride along at this speed for about a mile. If in close order, the command is: "Follow in order." [13] And they chase along with ranks close together.

To fall back a bit and then to wheel about, when the commander wants to fall back in open order he shouts: "Give way." [14] At a gallop the troops withdraw a bowshot or two toward the men in close order. He shouts again: "Turn. Threaten." [15] They then wheel around as though to face the enemy. They should practice this maneuver frequently, not only charging forwards, but also to the right and to the left, and as though they were heading toward the second line. In the intervals of that line, sometimes in the space between the lines, they should regroup and all together in irregular formation charge against the enemy. While drilling, the lances should be held high and not down to the side, so as not to impede the free movement of the horses.

To change front about to the left or to the right in an orderly manner, a necessary maneuver for the flank guards and the outflankers, the first command is: "To the left. Change front." [16] If to the right: "To the right. Change front." [17] And they change front. If only one bandon is involved, then that bandon changes front. But if there are several, then the one changes by itself, and the others conform to its movement.

The unit may be faced to the rear either by the men staying in position or by having them change the front of the battle line around. If a small enemy force suddenly attacks from the rear, the command is given: "About face." [18] Remaining in place each soldier turns to the rear, with only the officers and standard bearers actually moving around to the new front at the rear. If a large enemy force appears behind them, the order is: "Change place." [19] And the unit marches about by bandon.

12. *Cursu mina.*
13. *Cum ordine seque.*
14. *Cede.*
15. *Torna mina.*
16. *Depone senestra.*
17. *Depone dextra.*
18. *Transforma.*
19. *Transmuta.*

Drilling the tagma must not be limited to the formations in line shown in the diagrams, which pertain only to the main charge. But irregular formations should also be practiced, marching out straight ahead and in various circular movements, first by falling back and wheeling about, then by surprise attacks against the enemy, and finally by giving prompt support to units in trouble. If the tagmas acquire some proficiency in these maneuvers, they will be prepared to operate in close or in extended order, and to form for every eventuality. When such drills have been properly performed, the soldiers become very familiar with all or almost all of them, and these nine maneuvers prepare the tagmas for any emergency, whether they be detailed to fight in extended order, closed order, as flank guards, or as outflankers, for they will have become accustomed to all the formations. It is also essential, of course, that the bandons become used to drawing up and cooperating with one another, as in the full battle line, but in such a way as not to divulge all our formations to the enemy. Apart from actual battle, the army should never draw up in its full combat formation; that is, when it is just drilling it should not be formed in a first and second line, with flank guards, outflankers, troops hiding in irregular formation or in ambushes. These dispositions are matters of strategy rather than of tactics, and they ought not be made known ahead of time during drill, but should be decided on the spot to meet a specific need.

Whether a single bandon is being drilled, or a moira, a meros, or the entire front line, it should be drawn up in three parts. If it is a single bandon to be drilled by itself, most of the men should be formed in extended order. On the same line with them about ten horsemen should be drawn up in single file on each flank in close order. A few other soldiers, say ten, should take their position on the opposite front to represent the enemy so our men can give the impression of directing their charge against them. When the advance begins, the troops in extended order separate from their close-order support and move out rapidly as though to combat. After riding steadily forward for a mile or two, they turn back about half that distance, make three or four quick charges to the right and to the left, and then circle back again. After all this they gallop to their original position in the area between the two close-order groups, and together with them they ride as if to encounter a pursuing enemy.

The same sort of drill should also be practiced by the moiras.

Some of its bandons should form in extended order, some in close order. They should then exchange roles, those in extended order change to close order, and those in close order change to extended order, with the result that all of them will be prepared for whatever is called for. The same principles apply in drilling a meros, as well as the first and the second battle lines. When several bandons of troops in extended order are practicing encircling charges and are divided into two commands riding against one another, with one division charging outwards and the other inwards, great care should be taken to avoid collisions among the horsemen.

The flank guards and outflankers, along with those irregular groups hiding among them, must be drilled separately. When the enemy lines extend beyond ours on both sides, they should keep our line even and guard it against envelopment by the enemy. They should be trained in the appropriate encircling and enveloping maneuvers against enemy lines shorter than or equal to ours. A few horsemen, say one or two bandons, should line up opposite them in a single line as though they were the enemy, so that the outflankers conforming to the length of their line may first outflank them and then the irregular groups concealed among them can suddenly and swiftly charge out by themselves and fall upon the rear of the enemy.

These maneuvers are simple and can easily be practiced by a single tagma or by several combined without disclosing our order of battle to the enemy. The others described below are not as essential. These drills should be written down and given to the merarchs and moirarchs. They should be practiced not only on level ground, but also in difficult terrain, in hilly and steep country. Even in hot weather it is a good idea to drill and practice. Nobody knows what will happen.

6. *Formation of the Meros. Explanation of the Symbols Illustrating the Formation of the Meros and Its Personnel.*

ᓚ   The Merarch

ᒙ   The Moirarch

✝   Bandon in extended order

δ   Bandon in close order

ᚴ   Page of the Federati, when called for.

MEROS OF THE FEDERATI. FORMATION

moira in extended order	moira in close order	moira in extended order

7. Explanation of the Symbols Illustrating the Formation of the First and Second Lines

Φ The Lieutenant General

ð Medical corpsman

Ҡ Flank guard

ʊ̃ Outflanker

Ҟ Optimates' man-at-arms

λ Reserve horses, if present

Τ Baggage train, if present

Ϛ Bandon of the baggage train guard, if present

N̓ Taxiarch of the Optimates

க The General

42

8. Formation of the Entire Line of Battle When the Baggage Train Also Has to Be Present

FORMATION OF THE FIRST BATTLE LINE

flank guards, 1–3 banda	meros of Vexillations	meros of federati	meros of Illyrikiani	outflankers, 1–2 banda
ҡ ҡ ҡ	✝ѫ✝ ᴣᴣ ᴣ ᴣᴣᴧᴣ ᴣ ᴣ ᴣ✝ѫ✝	✝ѫ✝ ᴣᴣ ᴣ ᴣᴣ ᴏ ᴣᴣ ᴣ ᴣ✝ѫ✝	✝ѫ✝ ᴣᴣ ᴣ ᴣᴣᴧᴣ ᴣ ᴣ ᴣ✝ѫ✝	K K
K K K	K K K K K K K K K K K K K K K K	K K K K K K K K K K K K K K K K	K K K K K K K K K K K K K K K K	K K
K K K	K K K K K K K K K K K K K K K K	K K K K K K K K K K K K K K K K	K K K K K K K K K K K K K K K K	K K
K K K	K K K K K K K K K K K K K K K K	K K K K K K K K K K K K K K K K	K K K K K K K K K K K K K K K K	K K
K K K	K K K K K K K K K K K K K K K K	K K K K K K K K K K K K K K K K	K K K K K K K K K K K K K K K K	K K
K K K	K K K K K K K K K K K K K K K K	K K K K K K K K K K K K K K K K	K K K K K K K K K K K K K K K K	K K
K K K	K K K K K K K K K K K K K K K K	K K K K K K K K K K K K K K K K	K K K K K K K K K K K K K K K K	K K
ᴣ	ᴣ ᴣ ᴣ ᴣ ᴣ ᴣ	ᴣ ᴣ ᴣ ᴣ ᴣ ᴣ	K K K K K K K K K K K K K K K K	ᴣ
			ᴣ ᴣ ᴣ ᴣ ᴣ ᴣ	

SECOND, OR SUPPORT LINE

meros	tagma	meros	tagma	meros	tagma	meros
✝ѫ✝ᴣᴣᴧᴣ ᴣ✝ѫ✝	K K K K K K K K✝ѫ✝ᴣᴣ ꙮᴣ ᴣ✝ѫ✝	K K K ♣ K K K K✝ѫ✝ᴣᴣᴧᴣ ᴣ✝ѫ✝	K K K K K K K✝ѫ✝ᴣᴣᴧᴣ ᴣ✝ѫ✝			
K K K K K K K K K K K K K K K K K K K K K K K K K K K K K K K K K K K K K	K K K K K K K K K K K K K K K K K K K K K K K K K K K K K K K K K K K K K					
K K K K K K K K K K		K K K K K K K K K K		K K K K K K K K K K		K K K K K K K K K K
K K K K K K K K K K		K K K K K K K K K K		K K K K K K K K K K		K K K K K K K K K K
K K K K K K K K K K		K K K K K K K K K K		K K K K K K K K K K		K K K K K K K K K K
K K K K K K K K K K		K K K K K K K K K K		K K K K K K K K K K		K K K K K K K K K K
K K K K K K K K K K		K K K K K K K K K K		K K K K K K K K K K		K K K K K K K K K K

rearguard	baggage train	reserve horses, 1	rearguard
K ᴣ K	ꝩ T T T T T	ʌ ʌ ʌ ʌ ʌ ʌ ʌ	K ᴣ K
K K K	T T T T T	ʌ ʌ ʌ ʌ ʌ ʌ ʌ	K K K
K K K	T T T T T	ʌ ʌ ʌ ʌ ʌ ʌ ʌ	K K K
K K K	T T T T T	ʌ ʌ ʌ ʌ ʌ ʌ ʌ	K K K
K K K	T T T T T		K K K

reserve horses, 2

ʌ ʌ ʌ ʌ ʌ ʌ ʌ
ʌ ʌ ʌ ʌ ʌ ʌ ʌ
ʌ ʌ ʌ ʌ ʌ ʌ ʌ

If the army happens to be over fifteen thousand strong, it is permissible and in fact advisable to organize the second line in four divisions with three spaces between them, as shown in the diagram, so that each meros of the first line may have its own space. If the army is of moderate strength, say from five or six to fifteen thousand, then

43

the second line should have two divisions and one clear space according to the second following diagram showing a single meros. If the army is even smaller, five thousand or less, then station one meros as the second line. The clear spaces in the second line between the divisions ought to be proportionate to the number of units drawn up in the first line, so that each space is one-fourth the width. That is, if the meros in the first line has six hundred cavalrymen across, the clear space in the second line should be about one hundred and fifty across. As mentioned above, the depth of the tagmas stationed in those clear spaces should ordinarily be four deep, so that, if necessary, they may also be available for offensive action. But if the army is of moderate strength, it suffices for them not to fight, but to remain and keep the second line intact.

9. A Single Meros

K K K K K K K K K K K K K K K K K K K K K K K K
K K K K K K K K K K K K K K K K K K K K K K K K
K K K K K K K K K K K K K K K K K K K K K K K K
K K K K K K K K K K K K K K K K K K K K K K K K
K K K K K K K K K K K K K K K K K K K K K K K K
K K K K K K K K K K K K K K K K K K K K K K K K
K K K K K K K K K K K K K K K K K K K K K K K K

SECOND LINE

K K K K K K   K K K K K K
K K K K K K   K K K K K K
K K K K K K   K K K K K K
K K K K K K   K K K K K K
            K K K K K K K K K K
            K K K K K K K K K K

44

Example of a single meros drawn up as previously described. If this meros should be driven back, it takes refuge in the second line. As it pulls back, it finds room in the middle, the standard bearer of the tagma or its commander giving the cry: "Admit."[20]

10. Formation of an Army of Moderate Strength

K K K K K K K K K   K K K K K K K K K   K K K K K K K K K
K K K K K K K K K   K K K K K K K K K   K K K K K K K K K
K K K K K K K K K   K K K K K K K K K   K K K K K K K K K
K K K K K K K K K   K K K K K K K K K   K K K K K K K K K
K K K K K K K K K   K K K K K K K K K   K K K K K K K K K
K K K K K K K K K   K K K K K K K K K   K K K K K K K K K
K K K K K K K K K   K K K K K K K K K   K K K K K K K K K
K K K K K K K K K   K K K K K K K K K   K K K K K K K K K

SECOND LINE

K K K K K K K K K K K K K
K K K K K K K K K K K K K
K K K K K K K K K K K K K
K K K K K K K K K K K K K
K K K K K K K K K K K K K

This plan with the second line consisting of one meros and no more is appropriate when the army is of moderate strength, that is, from two to five or six thousand and less. In case of emergency the first line should race to the ends or flanks of the second line, not to its front ranks. If the whole army consists of from five to ten or twelve thousand, the second line must be divided into two divisions with a clear space between them, as previously explained in the diagram of a single meros, and if the first line is driven back it can find refuge there. In dealing with fifteen or twenty thousand and more, the second line must consist of four divisions with three clear spaces, as

20. *Suscipe.*

explained in the chapter treating of that. This disposition of the line is essential when the army is exceptionally strong.

Disposition of flank guards and outflankers when the enemy battle line is longer or shorter than our own.

THE ENEMY BATTLE LINE

front

FORMATION OF THE FIRST BATTLE LINE WITH THE OUTFLANKERS CONCEALED UNTIL THE MOMENT OF CONTACT

flank guards   meros   meros   front   meros   outflankers

concealed droungos

enemy line

front

FORMATION OF THE FIRST BATTLE LINE WHEN THE HOSTILE LINE IS LONGER AND THERE IS NO TIME TO EXTEND OUR OWN RIGHT TO EQUAL IT

flank guards   meros   front   meros   meros   outflankers

If the enemy battle line is found to be considerably longer on both sides, our center, not the flanks, should advance to combat ahead of the other units.

46

ENVELOPMENT OF THE ENEMY WHEN THEIR LINE
IS SHORTER AT BOTH ENDS AND WHEN THE TWO
BATTLE LINES APPROACH ONE ANOTHER

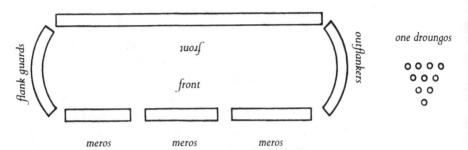

The troops preparing to launch an encircling or outflanking movement should slow down a bit to enable the flanks to get around the enemy line before making contact. If, on the other hand, our line is shorter and is being enveloped, then the troops of our second line who are following behind should attack the rear of the enveloping forces.

ENVELOPMENT WHEN THE LINES ARE OF EQUAL LENGTH

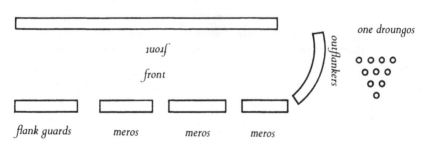

11. General Instructions

When the Roman forces have been organized and trained, first by tagma alone and then by meros, the officers of each meros should be called together and given the following basic instructions in writing. If rabbits or other small animals when pursued and hunted do not abandon themselves completely to headlong flight, but look back to observe how vigorously their attackers are chasing them and regulate their running away accordingly, how much more should men possessing intelligence and fighting for such a cause be careful in making their pursuits and withdrawals in battle. Like water which flows now forward now backward, they should not with every little advance made by the enemy or by themselves lose all control and take needless risks. But they should remain steadfast and strive in every conceivable way to defeat the enemy. For to push the enemy back a short distance and let them go is not a decisive victory, nor is it a defeat to fall back a bit and then make a stand again. But it is only when the war is ended that victory and defeat may be determined, and one must continue fighting toward that goal. To be really certain, then, that the officers understand the principles of the above formations and drills which contribute to the execution of these maneuvers, after the training of the individual units, the entire battle line should be formed once or at most twice and the principles illustrated by the maneuvers themselves.

12. Instructions for the Troops in the First Line

Orders should be given to the officers of the first or combat line to conform their movements to those of the center meros, where the lieutenant general is usually stationed. They should keep abreast of it and make their charge at the same time. If the enemy be driven back by the charge, then the assault troops should quickly chase after them continuing their pursuit right up to the enemy camp. The defenders should follow without halting and maintaining their formation. Then, in case the enemy wheels around and the assault troops cannot handle the fighting at close quarters, they can take refuge among the defenders and rally. If it happens during the battle that any one meros, or all of them, should be driven back, it should retreat as though upon the second line a bowshot or two and, the usual appropriate commands being shouted out, turn around again against the enemy. They may then be able to force the enemy to turn in flight, but if not, they should retire a bit and wheel around again. And if after one or two attempts they are still unsuccessful in driving the enemy back, then the second line should move up, the first taking

48

refuge behind it and filtering through the clear spaces in it, and in the area between the second and the third lines it should reform and attack the enemy in irregular formation together with the second line. If they turn, pursue them relentlessly.

13. Instructions for the Flank Guards

Orders should be given to the flank guards that if the enemy's flank extends beyond ours, they should make every effort, inclining to the flank, that is the shield, to extend our flank and make it equal, to prevent envelopment of the meros. But if it is shorter, they should hasten to advance in crescent formation and envelop it before the meros launches its attack, that is, just before the signal for the charge is given. If the lines are of equal length, they should stay in their own position in close order and join the rest of the meros in the charge.

14. Instructions for the Outflankers

Orders should be given to the outflankers that, until the enemy gets to about two or three bowshots from our battle line, they are, as explained, to follow along hidden behind the right wing. One tagma with its dekarchs and pentarchs should be posted in the front rank, for a depth of about five is enough if the troops are good. The other tagma should be stationed in irregular fashion behind the first. The standards, that is, their heads, should not be carried straight up, but lower, so as not to be seen and recognized by the enemy until the right moment. If the enemy's flank extends beyond ours, they first incline to the flank, that is, the lance, while the right meros slackens its pace a bit, and they extend their ranks to about half a bowshot until they outflank the opposing wing. While they are turning against and encircling it, the signal, "Head out," [21] is given, and the concealed droungos suddenly charges out from behind with great force and speed. If the enemy turns back in flight, they should not pursue them, but should join with the other tagma and immediately attack the rear of the remaining enemy units. But if the enemy line is shorter, they should immediately move out of the meros and in crescent formation envelop it. If the lines are of the same length, they should extend their ranks a bit to outflank the opposing wing and

21. *Exi.*

then, as said, charge. Now if, while the outflankers are extending their ranks, the enemy wants to extend theis in like manner, then they should immediately launch the charge against them while they are still moving about. For in turning by the flank the enemy will have to expose their right, and their formation will be loose. Not only must the outflankers regulate these circling movements so that they are not too slow nor too much ahead, but the commander of the whole meros must time its assault to coincide with the out-flankers' attacks as they begin to cause confusion among the enemy. His purpose should be to outflank the opposing meros if he can do so, otherwise he should at the very least extend his line to the same length. If the enemy battle line is longer, then he should aim at en-abling the outflankers to go about their task properly. It should be noted that the outflankers are essential because, as said, they can carry out surprise attacks with impunity even in open country.

15. Instructions for the Troops in the Second Line

Orders should be given to the second line to follow and conform its movements to those of the center unit in which the general normally takes his stand. At the moment in which the first line makes contact with the enemy, the second line should be about three or four bowshots behind it. If the enemy turns back, it should follow along in close-order support, maintaining its formation, and not halting. If our first line is defeated, the units driven back should be allowed to pass through the tagmas of the third line and find a place of safety. The second line should continue to advance in good order together with the troops of the first line and should not break formation until the final outcome of the battle and the return to camp. They should always maintain their formation and not become disordered in pur-suing the enemy.

Now, if the battle is in doubt as far as the first line is concerned, and first one side gains the advantage and then the other, then the second line is to wait and see how things turn out, letting out two or three rousing cheers to encourage our troops and discourage the enemy. They should be very careful not to engage in action pre-maturely or to get too close to the first line, which could result in confusion and a stupid defeat.

If it does happen that the second line is broken, it should retreat as far as the rear guard or the third line and set about reforming itself.

What if they hear that the enemy is attacking from some ambush to the rear? If it is only a small party, the troops in the third line should be able to deal with it, and they can be sent out against them. But if these are not strong enough by themselves, the men in the second line should turn around, the commanding officer with the standard marching to the rear, and with the line facing both ways they will easily be able to make their attack. If the enemy retreats, one or two bandons of the rear guard should attack them. If the enemy is reported to be numerous, give the command: "Countermarch." [22] In each tagma the dekarchs march to the rear, which then becomes the new front. Make it a standing order for all troops that nobody dare charge out in front of the second line even if the first line should be routed.

16. Instructions for Troops Assigned to an Ambush

Orders should be given to troops sent out to ambush or raid the enemy battle line that, first of all, patrols must be sent ahead so the detachment will not encounter an enemy force unexpectedly or an ambush from the flank or from the rear of the enemy battle line. For the enemy also frequently draws up their forces in two lines and, unless very carefully planned, our raids upon their first line may result in our own troops being ambushed by them. Therefore, if the enemy should also draw up in two lines, do not launch a raid against the rear of their first line, but against a flank or wing, whether the ambush, as mentioned, took place from one or both sides. Time this attack so that it does not occur too much in advance of that of our battle line nor too much after it. But when the two lines are about two or three bowshots apart, then the detachments sent out on ambush should assault the enemy. But if the men have been properly trained, as explained above, it will not be necessary to spend time on these instructions, for they will be able to deal with each situation as it arises.

22. *Transmuta.*

· B O O K   I V ·
Ambushes

1. Ambushes and Stratagems Against Superior Enemy Forces

Well-planned ambushes are of the greatest value in warfare. In various ways they have in a short time destroyed great powers before they had a chance to bring their whole battle line into action. Some commanders have availed themselves of favorable terrain, such as dense woods, valleys, steep hills, ravines, mountains extending almost up to the enemy battle line. They have used these to conceal troops and to keep them from being detected at a distance and attacked. Then, suddenly charging in on the enemy's rear before the main battle could begin, they threw them into disorder and routed them. Other commanders, when the terrain was not to their advantage, would not place the ambush close to the enemy line, but on the flank between the enemy lines and theirs or even behind their own flank. On occasion they would station the larger force in ambush and have a smaller force draw up as though to face the enemy. This is particularly useful against the light-haired and other undisciplined peoples.

2. The Scythian Ambush

Instead of a large number of troops, some commanders draw up the smaller part of the army. When the charge is made and the lines clash, those soldiers quickly turn to flight; the enemy starts chasing them and becomes disordered. They ride past the place where the ambush is laid, and the units in ambush then charge out and strike the enemy in the rear. Those fleeing then turn around, and the en-

52

emy force is caught in the middle. The Scythian peoples do this all the time.

3. Ambushes from Both Sides

Some commanders have dug a trench eight or ten feet deep, fifty or sixty wide, and extending a good distance. They covered this with light pieces of wood, with hay and earth, so it looked just like the ground around it, and there was no way you could tell the difference. The excavated earth was removed from the site, so that it would not look at all strange. At various places in the middle of the trench they left some solid crossings of firm ground, well marked and made known at the proper time to their own army. Near the trench on both sides they placed troops in ambush under cover where they could not be seen, and they drew up the rest before the trench. When battle was joined, the men drawn up before the trench simulated defeat, retiring safely back over the solid sections known to them. The enemy began an unrestrained, impetuous pursuit and fell into the trench. Then the soldiers posted in ambush suddenly charged out, and the men who had feigned retreat turned back. Most of the enemy perished, some falling into the trench, others while fleeing in disorder because of the unexpected disaster. It was by this stratagem that the Nephthalites defeated Peroz, King of the Persians.[1]

This type of ambush, however, requires a good deal of time and many laborers, and it can easily be discovered by the enemy through deserters or scouts. The same sort of thing has been done by using swampy ground. The commander locates two or three solid and firm passageways ahead of time and makes them known to his army when it is drawn up in formation. The troops are lined up in front of the swamp and, when the action begins, they feign flight, heading over the passageways, and lead the enemy to fall right into the swamp. Then the troops in ambush on the flanks suddenly charge upon them, and the men feigning retreat overpower and destroy the enemy. The Scythian tribes of the Goths used this against the Roman emperor Decius when they crossed the Danube and invaded Thrace

1. In A.D. 468: Agathias, *Historiarum libri*, 4, 27, 4; Procopius, *De bello Persico*, 1, 4.

and waged open war against him around Moesia.[2] Up to that time Decius himself had been successfully employing the same strategy, simulated retreat, in intensive warfare which enabled him to destroy many of them.

This same kind of trap may be laid for the enemy without a trench or swamp. At a time when it will not be noticed, iron caltrops can be scattered or placed in position, strung together so they can easily be collected after being used. They should extend the whole length of the battle line to a depth of a hundred feet. Four or five passageways should be left in the middle, about three or four hundred feet wide, known to our army and clearly marked by large tree branches, spear heads with odd shapes, heaps of earth or stones, or other obvious marks. These should be placed not only just at the entrances of the passages or the front of the area covered by the caltrops, but also in depth so that after the action begins, when the units feigning flight have passed through those passageways, the markers may be removed or overturned by riders assigned for this purpose. The soldiers in ambush on both sides may then charge out while the enemy is tripping over the caltrops and finding it difficult to move either forward or backward.

The same sort of thing can be done without the use of caltrops. Here and there round pits can be dug, of the type called "horse-breakers." They should be about one foot in diameter, two or three feet deep, with sharp stakes set in the bottom. These should be dug in alternating rows, not in straight lines, about three feet apart in all directions, and should cover an area of a hundred and fifty feet as long as the line of battle. When it is time for battle, now, the first line should draw up about a mile in front of these obstacles, and the second line about two or three bowshots behind the obstacles, not along the whole front but in line with the gaps or clear spaces. In an emergency, then, when the troops in the first line are driven back, they can safely retreat through those gaps and, if necessary, the second line may safely advance through the same gaps to attack the enemy. If the entire battle line is drawn up behind the obstacles, with no units in front, the line should be about three bowshots behind it. When the enemy advance gets to the obstacles, then charge out against them just as their horses are falling into the pits and being destroyed.

2. In A.D. 251 near the present Razgrad in the Dobrudja region of Rumania: Zosimus, *Historia*, 1, 23. The text incorrectly has Mysia, which was in northwest Asia Minor.

When our line is formed behind them, the clear spaces between the obstacles must not be very wide so that large numbers of the enemy may not be able to engage in the fighting without danger.

Any of these artifices or stratagems must be prepared secretly by a small group of reliable men. The work should be done on the very day of the battle or on the day before late in the evening and, of course, in that location in which the battle is expected, and there they should await the enemy. At the proper moment they should inform the soldiers, especially the standard bearers, so they may know what to do. In falling back they should not do so in their regular formation, but the bandons should follow in loose formation one behind the other according to the location of the clear spaces. All the soldiers must be ordered to follow their own standards, especially in falling back, lest, which God forbid, they wander about and themselves fall into the traps.

Of all the stratagems described above, it is our opinion that caltrops can more easily and with secrecy be employed on all sorts of ground. One must also, of course, form the battle line in accord with the terrain. If an assault upon the enemy line is decided on, as described in the previous book, about one or two bandons, even more depending on the size of the army, should be detailed, good soldiers under courageous and intelligent officers. Depending on the terrain, one group should undertake operations against the enemy line on its own right, and the other should do the same on the left. If the enemy launches an attack, these units should repulse it and not allow it time to reach and harass our battle line. If the enemy does not attack, then they themselves should attack in that sector or they should raid the enemy's baggage train if it should chance to be within reach, or the rear or wings of the enemy line. In case the enemy is formed in two lines or should have units for ambush behind its own line to find and injure our own ambushing parties, our men who have been detailed for ambush duty should keep up careful reconnaissance and so be prepared to meet any move by the enemy.

4. Timing of Ambushes

The time of the ambush should be carefully arranged. They should not make their attack too long before the main line for, being less numerous, they will be crushed by the enemy. Neither should they delay too long so that they show up after the main battle has begun and they accomplish nothing. The units detailed for ambuscades and the main body of the army should move at the same time, whether there is to be one ambush or two. Still, it is better to have the main body move out a bit before the ambush unit. The main battle line advances in the open and diverts the enemy's attention, while the other proceeds under cover. They should coordinate their movements by scouts, signals, and estimate. If one happens to get ahead by a short cut it should slow down and wait for the other one so that, if possible, both of them, the unit in ambush and the main battle line, should make contact with the enemy at the same time. Rather, the ambush unit should attack just a little before. The purpose of this is that when the enemy starts being thrown into disorder by the ambush, then the main line moves in and attacks. For the same reason, if the ground permits, ambushes should be made from both sides, especially if the army is large. One party may be used to repel assaults of the enemy, while the other attacks them. Then if one of them remains intact, even though their assaults may be unsuccessful or if in the meantime the main battle line is driven back, they should not for these reasons give in to the enemy, fall back on the second line and get mixed in with the fugitives, but they should keep clear and try to attack the enemy's rear and in this way rally their own men in flight.

5. Use of Irregular Formation by Troops Detailed for Ambushes and Surprise Attacks

We take it for granted that detachments designated for ambuscades, for attacks on the rear or the flanks of a line, for guarding the rear, the flanks, or the baggage train, for quick support to a unit which is hard pressed, or for minor reconnaissance are much better if they adopt an irregular formation rather than that appropriate for a large battle line, all arranged in dekarchies and pentarchies.[3] The line, it is true, looks impressive, is stronger, better ordered, and in battle can charge more securely, but since it is not very flexible, it is slow and awkward in maneuvering in emergencies. The irregular formation has the opposite characteristics. It can easily be concealed for an ambush; it does not require much room; and it can maneuver quickly in an emergency. For these reasons, time should be devoted to practicing it, and its basic elements will become obvious by experience it-

3. Irregular formation: *droungos*. Vegetius calls it a *globus: Ep. rei milit.*, 3, 19.

self. It should be adapted to the size of the detachment and to the lay of the land. If a very large or even moderate-sized unit of the main army is to be placed in ambush with the idea of attacking in one place, it should be formed by dekarchies or pentarchies. But if only a few troops are involved or the attack is at different points, then the irregular formation is called for. In other words, the difference between the two formations is this: the first is for major operations involving little risk; the other is for quick support, pursuit, sudden raids, and causing confusion. This latter formation, regarded as appropriate for cavalry, should be learned by constant drill in the manner we have described by the individual bandons. If the skills are acquired properly, there will be no need for instructions or any other orders. The formation itself and the drill teach each man what he has to do.

Some people, overcautious and hesitant to change, might argue that this formation is rather complicated and variable and is consequently too much trouble. Those people ought to realize that athletes, charioteers, and others who compete in mere amusements do so only for material success and reward, and a very mediocre one at that, and the only penalty for failure is their own chagrin, but they subject themselves to so much hardship and labor. They rigidly restrict their diet and never cease training so they might learn various ways of injuring their adversaries, ways of keeping themselves from being injured by them, and how to break the holds they might be caught in. How much the more, then, ought we to practice these formations and drills tirelessly, with flexibility, and with intelligence? In this case failure means swift death or flight, which is worse than death, whereas success brings gratification, material gain, fame, eternal memory. We should not rely on just one formation, since one accidental mistake means the lives of so many men. The one responsible may never be known, but for the mistake of one man all must suffer. Since there is no need to write about this at length, even listing the reasons would make the book too long. It is much more work to read about these drills than to do them.

· B O O K   V ·
On Baggage Trains

1. Caution in Leading the Baggage Train onto the Battlefield

The baggage train must be regarded as essential and should never be neglected. It should not haphazardly be left behind without protection nor, on the other hand, should it carelessly be brought onto the battlefield. For included with the train are the servants needed by the soldiers, their children and other members of their families. If their safety is not assured, the soldiers become distracted, hesitant, and dispirited in battle. For an intelligent man makes an effort to profit at the enemy's expense without any harm to himself. First of all, we advise that no large number of servants be brought into the area where the main battle is expected, whether this be in our own country or off in a foreign one, but only a moderate number, and vigorous men at that. There should be enough servants to each squad to take care of their horses, in proportion to the different ranking of the units or the number of horses, so as to avoid a lot of confusion, inopportune expense, and distraction among them. At the time of battle these servants should be left behind in the camp, whether the battle is fought in our own or in foreign territory, and any infantry units which may be present should join the troops assigned to the train. This is to be done carefully, as explained in the section on camps.

2. Reserve Horses

The reserve horses should also be left with the baggage train. We cannot think of any reason why the soldiers have their servants lead along all the reserve horses on the day of battle. For whether the army wins or loses, there is so much tension, disorder, and confusion that in such a mob nobody could recognize his reserve horse and hope to mount it. This was one of the good reasons we had in providing for the medical corpsmen to aid in such circumstances. In small raiding or scouting parties the soldiers must have spare horses, which must be kept healthy and in good condition up to the very day of battle. But once the battle begins, it is our considered judgment that there is no need to have the reserve horses near the battle line; instead, they should be left in the camp. For they can easily become very confused when handled only by young boys.

3. Unnecessary Baggage

If the infantry is present, and if battle appears imminent, whether in our own country, a friendly one, or right on the frontier, and there is no chance of delay, then in a strong place about thirty or fifty miles away where grass and water are sufficient, leave the greater nonessential part of the baggage train and the extra horses, tools, and the rest of the equipment which is not needed on the day of battle. It should be guarded by one or two bandons, and they should be ordered to gather forage for four or five days, and to guard the horses within the enclosure until the battle is over. A few good men whom everyone knows should be chosen and stationed at intervals between this place and the front. They should report to the one in charge of the baggage train. Depending on how the battle goes, they should advise the troops in the train to remain in the same place where they were left, to move to another suitable place, or to rejoin the main army.

4. Intermediate Camps

Troops moving from that base camp up to combat should take with them their spare horses, small tents or a couple of heavy cloaks, the one for covering if needed and the other as a tent or shelter, also twenty or thirty pounds of hardtack, flour, or some other provisions of that sort, especially if they are going to fight the Scythians. They should also set up a suitable camp closer to the enemy. Fortifications should be constructed about this camp, even though the army might stay there only for a day. Each bandon should store there a day's supply of forage or hay. In case the army suffers a reverse in battle and has to beat a hasty retreat, it will have the option of staying in the camp itself, whether there be one or two of them, and it will have a day's provisions for its horses and not be forced to search for fodder and grass in the midst of such confusion and run the risk of being hurt if it searches about for provisions with the enemy all about or be forced to march on without provisions. Still, in case the army should move on without using the supplies, some men should be assigned to burn the fodder and then rejoin the main body.

5. Guarding the Baggage Train on the March

On the march when the enemy is nearby, the baggage train must always be in the middle, so it may not be subject to harassment for lack of protection. Troops on the march should not be mixed in or confused with the train, but they must be kept apart. The train should proceed by itself behind its own meros, and the soldiers should travel light by themselves.

End of the fifth book.

· B O O K   V I ·
Various Tactics and Drills

Constant drill is of the greatest value to the soldier. It is easy, however, for the enemy to learn what is going on through spies and deserters, and as a result all the practice is useless. Actually, the drill
described above is sufficient, for its simplicity makes it adaptable to
any formation without disclosing our whole plan of battle. Still, if
there is the opportunity for more sophisticated drill, each meros in-
dividually should practice various formations and drills, first the one
given below for actual use and then those additional ones which are
not really essential. Each formation or drill should be identified in a
special way, so the soldiers who are trained in these maneuvers may
recognize the differences and not be puzzled by them, and also that
they may not know what plan the general intends to follow when the
time comes for battle. Now then, there are three simulated formations: the Scythian, the Alan, the African; and one for actual use,
the Italian.

1. The Scythian Drill, Simulated

The Scythian formation is one in which the tagmas are all formed in
the same manner, as in former times, not with some of them arranged as assault troops and some as defenders. They should be
drawn up in one line, divided into two moiras instead of the usual
three. The two flanks of the meros move out as though beginning an
encircling maneuver, advancing toward one another, and surrounding an open space. Continuing along in a circle, the right wing on the
outside, the left on the inside, they ride into the opposite section of
one another's line. This used to be part of the cavalry games in winter
quarters during March.[1]

1. The Life of St. Anastasius the Persian (*Acta S. Anastasii Persae*, ed. H. Usener,

2. The Alan Drill, Simulated

In the Alan system the troops, some as assault and some as defenders, are drawn up in a single battle line. This is divided into moiras, lined up about two or four hundred feet from each other. The assault troops advance at a gallop as if in pursuit, and then turn back filtering into the intervals or clear spaces in the main line. Then, together with the defenders they turn and charge against the enemy. In another maneuver the assault troops turn around in those intervals and charge out against both flanks of the unit, the men keeping their original relative positions.

3. The African Drill, Simulated

In the African system the troops are drawn up in one battle line, which has been the usual practice until the present. The middle moira is composed of defenders, both wings of assault troops. In picking up speed, as though in pursuit, the center moira drops behind a bit maintaining its close-order formation, while the assault troops on both flanks begin to move out. Then, when it is time to turn back, one moira stays in position or slows down on the outside, while the other races back to the defenders. The wing which had halted then starts moving back to the main line; the other wing moves quickly out to meet it, riding off to one side, and in this way the two wings come face to face, but without colliding. There is another formation similar to this in which the troops are drawn up in the opposite way; that is, the central moira consists of assault troops, and the wings of defenders, but following the same movements. To be correct, it should be called the Illyrikian system.

4. The Italian Drill, for Actual Use

The Italian system is both a formation and a drill which, in our opinion, is suitable for use against any people. It consists of two lines, a front line and a support, with assault troops and defenders, with flank guards, outflankers, and detachments for ambush, all of which has been explained above and illustrated by diagrams.

Programma Universitatis Bonnae [1884], 13) reports: "During the month of March it has long been traditional for the soldiers to equip their horses, ride them out to the plain, and exercise them as though training for warfare."

In general, we should practice these various systems of drill, so others will not find out which one we think is more important. Or, when the front line is being drilled, the second line should not be on the field with it, but just the first line, and that without its flank guards, outflankers, and ambush detachments. This strikes us as the simplest and most basic plan. Moreover, in place of a second line a few cavalrymen can stand there to represent it, so the troops in the first line may become accustomed to the distance to cover in seeking safety. Likewise, the second line may be drilled by itself with a few troops stationed on the site of the first line, so the second may get used to providing refuge for the first line when necessary.

5. Drilling the Outflankers and Flank Guards

Flank guards and outflankers may be drilled separately in their own formations before wartime so they may become accustomed to the movements involved without disclosing them. First, the outflankers may be stationed under cover behind the right flank, or they may be drawn up on the flank even with the line. Either way, when it is time for their enveloping movement, they incline to the right and then ride out as far as necessary. Maintaining formation, they quickly return to their original position in such a way as to envelop the enemy line at the same time. Similarly the flank guards, posted by the left meros, incline to the left, ride out as far as necessary, quickly return to their original position in such a way as to make our line equal in extent to that of the enemy.

· B O O K   V I I ·
Strategy. The Points Which the General Must Consider

BEFORE THE DAY OF BATTLE

A ship cannot cross the sea without a helmsman, nor can one defeat an enemy without tactics and strategy. With these and the aid of God it is possible to overcome not only an enemy force of equal strength but even one greatly superior in numbers. For it is not true, as some inexperienced people believe, that wars are decided by courage and numbers of troops, but, along with God's favor, by tactics and generalship, and our concern should be with these rather than wasting our time in mobilizing large numbers of men. The former provide security and advantage to men who know how to use them well, whereas the other brings trouble and financial ruin.

The leader must take advantage of favorable times and places in fighting against the enemy. First, he must guard against hostile attacks which can injure our men, and then he must attempt to launch the same against the enemy. Above all he must look for enemy ambushes, sending out frequent and far-ranging patrols in all directions in the area around the battlefield. He must avoid disordered and uncoordinated pursuits. We would not allow the general to take part personally in raids or other reckless attacks. These should be entrusted to other competent officers. For if one of the subordinate officers blunders or fails, the situation may be quickly straightened out. But if the leader of the whole army fails, his fall can open the way to complete disorder.

That general is wise who before entering into war carefully studies the enemy, and can guard against his strong points and take advantage of his weaknesses. For example, the enemy is superior in cavalry; he should destroy his forage. He is superior in number of troops; cut off their supplies. His army is composed of diverse peoples; corrupt them with gifts, favors, promises. There is dissension among them; deal with their leaders. This people relies on the spear; lead them into difficult terrain. This people relies on the bow; line up in the open and force them into close, hand-to-hand fighting. Against Scythians or Huns launch your assault in February or March when their horses are in wretched condition after suffering through the winter, and proceed as just suggested for attacking archers. If they march or make camp without proper precautions, make unexpected raids on them by night and by day. If they are reckless and undisciplined in combat and not inured to hardship, make believe you are going to attack, but delay and drag things out until their ardor cools, and when they begin to hesitate, then make your attack on them. The foe is superior in infantry; entice him into the open, not too close, but from a safe distance hit him with javelins.

Warfare is like hunting. Wild animals are taken by scouting, by nets, by lying in wait, by stalking, by circling around, and by other such stratagems rather than by sheer force. In waging war we should proceed in the same way, whether the enemy be many or few. To try simply to overpower the enemy in the open, hand to hand and face to face, even though you might appear to win, is an enterprise which is very risky and can result in serious harm. Apart from extreme emergency, it is ridiculous to try to gain a victory which is so costly and brings only empty glory.

1. Blessing the Flags

A day or two before hostilities begin, the merarchs should see that the flags are blessed and then present them to the standard bearers of the tagmas.

2. Organization of the Squads

The commanding officer of each tagma should organize it into squads and keep them at full strength.

3. Gathering Intelligence About the Enemy

Every effort should be made by continuously sending out keen-sighted scouts at appropriate intervals, by spies and patrols, to obtain information about the enemy's movements, their strength and organization, and thus be in a position to prevent being surprised by them.

4. Using Speeches to Encourage the Troops

At some convenient time the troops should be assembled by meros or moira, not all at once in one place. Suitable speeches should be given to encourage them, recalling their former victories, promising rewards from the emperor, and recompense for their loyal service to the state. Written orders should then be communicated by the proper officers to each tagma.

5. Enemy Prisoners Taken by Patrols

If some of the enemy are captured by a patrol or desert to us, then, if they are nicely armed and in good physical condition, they should not be shown to the army, but sent off secretly to some other place. But if they appear in miserable shape, make sure to show the deserters to the whole army; have the prisoners stripped and paraded around, and make them beg for their lives so that our men may think that all the enemy soldiers are that wretched.

6. Punishment of Offenders

In the vicinity of the enemy and with a pitched battle imminent, the commanding officers of the tagmas should be ordered to guard against punishing soldiers who have committed offenses for those few days and not to deal harshly with the soldiers at all. Instead, they should be careful in dealing with those who are suspected of harboring some grievance. But if they prove intractable, then use some plausible pretext to send them off to some other place for a while until after the battle so they will not go over to the enemy and provide him with some information he should not have. Men of the same race as the enemy should be sent away long before and should not be brought into battle against their own people.

7. Maintenance of the Soldiers, Their Horses, and Their Camps

When battle is imminent, provisions should be made bearing in mind the possibility of defeat and steps taken to guard against its adverse effects. In particular, food for a few days for both men and horses should be collected. Fortified camps should be constructed in suitable places, according to the plan given below, in which water may be safely stored for emergencies.

8. Consultation with the Merarchs About the Field of Battle

The general should assemble the merarchs and make plans for the battle, giving attention to the location where the fighting is to take place.

9. Watering the Horses

Orders should be given early to the officers that at the first sound of the trumpet on the night before the day of battle they should make sure to lead the horses to water. If they neglect this, their men may be left behind when the time comes to form for combat.

10. Rations Carried in Saddlebags

Orders are to be given each soldier that when he moves up to his place in line he should carry in his saddlebags a pound or two of bread, barley, boiled meal, or meat, and in a little sack a small flask of water, not wine. These may be needed in victorious circumstances as well as in others which may occur. For often enough a defeated enemy races back to a fortified position, and it is necessary to spend the night there, or to lay in wait for them, or to continue the battle until evening. Rations must then be provided so that operations need not be broken off because of lack of them.

11. Waging War Against an Unfamiliar People

If we find ourselves at war with a powerful people and one whose ways are strange to us, and the army, not knowing what to expect becomes nervous, then we must be very careful to avoid getting into an open battle with them right away. Before any fighting the first and the safest thing to do is to choose a few experienced and lightly armed soldiers and have them very secretly carry out attacks against some detachments of the enemy. If they succeed in killing or capturing some of them, then most of our soldiers will take this as evidence of our own superiority. They will get over their nervousness, their morale will pick up, and they will gradually become used to fighting against them.

12. Surprise Attacks by the Enemy on the March

If the enemy launches a surprise attack, and conditions are not favorable for battle because the terrain is rugged or thickly covered or because the time is not to our advantage, then we should not plan on fighting there. Instead, we should work on getting our forces together, occupy a position suitable for camp, and delay until the place and the time become more favorable and not be forced to fight when we do not want to. This does not mean that we are running away from the enemy, but only that we are avoiding a poor location.

13. Camps and Maintenance of the Horses in Them

When the enemy is approaching our camp, and especially if it looks as though the fighting is to be done in the Scythian manner, our options are as follows. If the army is to stay within the fortifications and there await the enemy, enough hay or grass for the horses for one or two days should be gotten ready and stored. But if the army is to march out with the idea of moving to another camp and there lining up for battle, then it has to carry along a day's supply of hay or grass and deposit it in the new fortification. For it is not likely that the enemy will allow the servants to go out foraging on that day or to graze the horses. But if the enemy should come very close, it would be a good idea, as mentioned, for each man to collect the necessary forage on the march. For usually after they have set up camp the boys will not be able to go out and collect forage, especially if the enemy cavalry outnumbers ours.

14. Not Stripping Enemy Corpses During the Fighting

To plunder the dead or to attack the baggage train or camp of the enemy before the battle is entirely over is very dangerous and can be disastrous. The soldiers should be warned well ahead of time, as is made clear in the military code, that they must absolutely avoid such acts. Often enough this sort of thing has caused troops who have already won a battle to be defeated and even annihilated. After they have scattered around, they have been wiped out by the enemy.

15. Peoples Akin to the Enemy

Long before battle, troops of the same race as the enemy should be separated from the army and sent elsewhere to avoid their going over to the enemy at a critical moment.

POINTS TO BE OBSERVED
ON THE DAY OF BATTLE

1. Not Overburdening the General on the Day of Battle

On the actual day of battle the general should not take on too many tasks. He might exert himself too much, become worn out, and overlook some really essential matters. He should not look downcast or worried but should ride jauntily along the lines and encourage all the troops. He should not himself join in the actual fighting; this is not the role of the general but of the soldier. After making all the proper arrangements, he should station himself in a suitable spot from which he can observe which troops are exerting themselves and which might be slackening. When needed he should be ready to send assistance to a unit in trouble by making use of his reserves, that is, the flank and rear guards.

2. Enemy Archers

In combat against archers every effort should be made to guard against positioning our troops on the lower slopes of mountains and difficult terrain. Our troops should form high up in the hills or else come down from the mountains all the way and draw up on level, open ground. Otherwise, they may be suddenly overcome by hostile detachments lying in ambush under cover of the heights.

3. Not Engaging the Enemy in Combat or Showing Our Own Strength Before Learning the Enemy's Intentions

Contact should not be made with the enemy's main body, nor should they be allowed to observe our own formation clearly, before reconnoitering their lines and finding out whether they are planning any ambushes.

4. Concealment of the Second Line When It Is Unable to Follow Behind the First So That the Two Appear as One

If the site of the battle is in open and unobstructed country in which the second line cannot be easily hidden, then, to keep the enemy from accurately observing the army as it advances to combat, the second line should follow very closely behind the first so that the two will appear as one battle line to the enemy. About a mile away from them our second line should slow down, gradually drop behind the first line to the proper distance, and assume its normal formation. This makes it difficult for the enemy, or even for our own allies, to get a clear idea of how we are disposing our troops.

5. Intelligence and Method of Meeting a Surprise Enemy Attack

If it is reported that an enemy detachment has gotten by our flank guards and our own ambushing parties and is launching an attack against our front line, then some of the bandons stationed on the flanks of our second line should come to their support. If they attack from one side, the support should come from that flank; if from both sides, then from both flanks. If the attack is directed against the rear of the second line, and the rear guard is not strong enough to deal with it, the same flank units should provide aid. In this way the rest of the troops can concentrate on their duty of supporting the first line.

6. The Wounded

After the battle the general should give prompt attention to the wounded and see to burying the dead. Not only is this a religious duty, but it greatly helps the morale of the living.

7. Apparent Strength of the Enemy

If the enemy's army is large and appears formidable by reason of the multitudes of men and horses, we should not draw up our army on high ground right away while the enemy is still at a distance. Apprehensive at the sight of such a large force, our men will quickly begin to lose courage. Instead, they should be formed on lower ground where they will not see the enemy or be seen by them. When the enemy approaches to about a mile or half a mile, then the army should move to high ground, so that the troops will not have time to lose confidence before the battle begins. But if the terrain will not allow this strategy, and the enemy can be clearly seen from a distance, then spread the report beforehand along the battle line that the opposing force consists mostly of horses and baggage trains, not of men.

8. Preventing Hostile Reconnaissance of Our Line

One or two bandons should always be kept a mile or two in front of the main body before combat while the troops are forming their lines. This is to prevent the enemy from observing our formation and modifying theirs accordingly.

9. Guarding the Camp

If the army does not have many infantry, the soldiers' servants should be left behind, stationed along the length of the fortification, each one assigned a guard post along the inner ditch and provided with a weapon he can handle, bow, javelin, or sling. A bandon should stay with them to patrol and to guard the gates of the camp, and a competent officer should be placed in command of the whole camp.

The baggage train should never be brought out to the front line. During a battle it is too easy a prey for the enemy. Now if it happens that the enemy makes a surprise attack on our troops on the march and there is no time to set up camp and, as explained, secure our baggage train, then it should be stationed with the units on the right flank of the second line, and one or two bandons from whatever troops are available should be detailed to guard it.

10. Gathering Fodder

If it has not been possible to gather a supply of fodder beforehand, as recommended, then, on the day of battle, as the young men, that is, the soldiers are moving into formation, the servants should go out to collect it in the area to the rear of the battle line or of the camp. They should be accompanied by a few patrols taken from the troops left behind to guard the camp. While the battle is in progress they should be able to gather enough fodder. The servants should also be instructed that they are to watch for a signal given from certain high and conspicuous places to let them know that some of the enemy may be approaching. This may be a smoke signal or the blowing of a trumpet, that is, the signal for recall. When it is given, they are to return as fast as they can and take refuge in the camp, so they may not be cut off outside.

All this is essential because the outcome of the action is uncertain. In case of defeat, if the soldiers have provisions for themselves and their horses, they can choose to hold their position, to renew the fighting, or to retreat immediately in good order, as long as their horses are still in good condition, before the men lose their spirit or the horses their strength. But if provisions are not kept in readiness, then after a defeat nobody dares go out to gather fodder, with the result that the horses lose strength and the soldiers their spirit. Hunger and fear crush any ability to plan to improve the situation. It is absolutely essential to plan ahead and keep on hand food for the horses for one or two days, or more if it can be done, even if there should be good grazing near the camp.

11. After a Defeat

If the first day of battle ends in a defeat, it is, in our opinion, absolutely undesirable and useless to try to get those same troops who have been beaten in the field to go back into actual combat around the same time or within the next few days. We strongly advise any general against even thinking of doing this. It is an extremely difficult thing for anyone to bring off. Nobody makes a habit of immediately retrieving a defeat, except the Scythians, and it is particularly foreign to the Romans. For even if the general understands the mistake he has made and hopes to remedy it by means of a second battle, the soldiers as a whole are unable to grasp the reason for deliberately going right back into the fighting. They are more likely to look upon what happened as God's will and completely lose heart. So then, unless it is absolutely necessary, for a few days after a defeat in battle no attempt should be made to line up again and resume the offensive. It is better to rely on stratagems, deception, carefully timed surprise moves, and the so-called fighting while fleeing, until the troops come to forget their discouragement, and their morale picks up once more.

If the army is found to be in good spirits, and for good reasons, which would be difficult to enumerate here, the general thinks that another attack would be to his advantage, he should have the shattered first line become the second, and make the second into the first, retaining selected tagmas of the former first line, since the second by itself is smaller and would be too weak.

When a battle ends in defeat there must be no indecision or delay, unless of course there is reason to hope for the arrival of allies or some other form of support, or unless, as may happen, overtures have been made by the enemy. These must not be made public without good reason, but should be dealt with privately. If the terms are lenient, and what is proposed can be done immediately, agreement should not be put off but should be confirmed with hostages or by oath. But if the terms are harsh and proposed with a view to delaying and getting our troops to let up their guard, this should be countered by circulating rumors making them even more unfavorable, so that when the men learn how harsh they are they will become angry and feel compelled to resist the enemy more forcefully and be more obedient to their own officers. The greater the delay, the more demoralized do the vanquished become and the more confident the victors. Therefore, before the men become utterly depressed, the general should have the tagmatic commanders, as well as the dekarchs and pentarchs, exhort the troops and point out that this is no time for despondency but rather for anger against the enemy and for courage for all to make up for the failure of a few. If there is cause to hope that the defeat may be retrieved in the open field, the formations described should be used. But even if such is not the case, it is very important to show a bold front before the dangers. If the victorious foe consists mostly of infantry, then we should withdraw without delay on horseback and in good order either to retreat or to establish camp safely someplace else. If the victors consist of cavalry, Persians or Scythians, for example, it is best to abandon superfluous property and the slower horses. Except for a small mounted force, all should take their stand on foot in two phalanxes or formations, or in one four-sided rectangular formation. In the middle should be the horses and baggage, with the soldiers on the outside, as described, and the archers on foot in front of them. In this way the army can move or retreat in safety.

12. After a Victory in Battle

Correspondingly, if the outcome of the battle is favorable, one should not be satisfied with merely driving the enemy back. This is a mistake made by inexperienced leaders who do not know how to take advantage of an opportunity, and who like to hear the saying: "Be victorious but do not press your victory too hard."[1] By not seizing the opportunity, these people only cause themselves more trouble and place the ultimate results in doubt. There can be no rest until the enemy is completely destroyed. If they seek refuge behind fortifications, apply pressure by direct force or by preventing them from getting more supplies for men and horses until they are annihilated or else agree to a treaty to our advantage. One should not slacken after driving them back just a short distance, nor, after so much hard work and the dangers of war, should one jeopardize the success of the whole campaign because of lack of persistence. In war, as in hunting, a near-miss is still a complete miss.

Especially after a victory, careful attention should be paid to maintaining good order among the soldiers. Still, although much has been written about such order, by itself it is not enough to assure one's own safety and to damage the enemy, but, after the assistance of God, the primary, essential factor is the general's management of the war. He must take full advantage of times and places. If, for example, he decides on getting into a pitched battle, he must look over every suitable location to find one which is open and level for his lancers. Not only must patrols be sent out to observe the sectors to the right, the left, and in the rear to a distance of two or three miles from the front until the end of the battle, but all the ground in front also in case there are any ditches or other traps.

13. Reconnaissance

On the day of battle, the patrols, mentioned above, which should be doubled, ought to head out early in the morning for two or three miles in every direction from the place where the fighting is expected to occur. They should have orders not only to observe the movements of the enemy and to report them, but also to stop any of

1. This proverb is quoted by Leo (*Tactical Constitutions*, 14, 25) and by Attaliotes as a well-known one: *Michaelis Attaliotae Historia*, ed. I. Bekker (Bonn, 1853), 26, 17. But its source is unknown.

our men trying to desert to the enemy. For out there they can easily intercept deserters from our army. Also in case any enemy soldiers with their possessions are coming over to our side, the patrols can provide them with safe conduct and keep them from being waylaid by any hoodlums who may be around.

The patrols covering the area in front of our main body should work their way to a bowshot from the enemy line opposite ours and see whether the enemy is secretly digging any ditches or planning some other trap, and so keep our own men from unexpected disaster. In unfavorable ground or in critical moments a single patrol must never be sent, but a second should cover the same ground. Then, in case one is captured, the other following behind will know about it. If our lines are ready and the terrain suitable, we should not wait for the enemy, allowing them time to adapt their formation to deal with ours, but the safest thing is to launch our attack immediately.

14. Not Exposing Our Second Line Too Soon

In case the main charge should be delayed for a good reason, the second line in particular must be kept hidden, in the woods if there are any about or in lower ground to the rear. If the enemy observes it too soon, they will be able to deal with it and neutralize it by means of ambushes and other stratagems.

15. Keeping the Polished Surface of the Weapons from Being Seen Before Battle

We find that the Romans and almost all other peoples when observing each other's battle lines from a distance generally pick out the gloomy-looking line as more likely to win the battle than the one in gleaming armor. This common view is clearly wrong for, after the judgment of God, battle is decided by the leadership of the general and the morale of the troops. Be this as it may, the authorities say that if woods or hollows are found in the vicinity, the army should be concealed in them and not be visible to the enemy long enough so that they will not be able to organize countermeasures; this would be until they are a mile or two away. If the ground is open and the air is clear, then the men should be trained not to wear their helmets but to carry them in their hands until very close to the enemy. If their shields are small, they should be carried on the chest to cover their mail coats, and their cloaks should be thrown back over the shoulder pieces of the mail coat until the proper time. The points of their lances should also be hidden. In this way, then, from a distance our army will not shine at all. Finally, by presenting such an appearance, something our foes also make use of, they will be impressed and even before the battle, will lose confidence.

16. Recapitulation of the Duties Assigned to Each Merarch

One-third of each meros should consist of assault troops and be posted on both flanks of the meros; the other two-thirds in the center should be defenders. Pennons should not be attached to the lances at the time of the charge, but should be removed and put in their cases. They may be carried on the lances until the enemy is about a mile away, and then they should be folded up. The standards of the tagmas should be on the small side, those of the moirarchs larger and of a different pattern, and in like manner that of the merarch should clearly stand out from the others. The "Nobiscum" should not be shouted during the charge, but only while moving up to the line of battle. As the charge begins, the troops, particularly those in the rear, should cheer and shout, and no other noise is needed. A number of trumpets should not be sounded in action; that of the merarch is sufficient. The merarch should station himself in the middle of the center meros, among the defenders. The moirarchs should be in the middle of the meros on either side, among the bandons of assault troops. It is the responsibility of the commanding officer of each moira and tagma to see that the men serving under him are prepared to observe all the regulations listed here.

When the lines are being formed, heralds should scout the area where the battle is expected, that is, the ground between our lines and the enemy. They should be on the lookout for ditches, swampy ground, or any traps which may have been laid. If any such are found, our lines should stay put, allow the enemy to advance past those spots, and then charge over good ground. Not only should the merarch's own standard be different in appearance from the others under his command, so as to be easily recognized by all subordinate standard bearers, but when the army halts, it should be carried in some distinctive way, such as a steady holding high or low, inclined to the right or the left, or raising up the head of the banner, or holding it upright and waving it frequently. In this way, even in the confusion of battle, it will be easily recognized by the other standards. The standards of all the merarchs must not be carried in the same way, but each should be different, and it should be practiced during drill, so that all the men may become familiar with them. Not only does this help the various bandons under the merarch's command to locate their own meros quickly, but it makes it easy for any stragglers, recognizing the standard of the meros to which they belong, also to find their own tagma.

Men of the same race as the enemy should be segregated before the day of battle and sent elsewhere on some plausible pretext. As noted, the merarch should have in writing the plans for the combined drilling of all the tagmas of the meros.

17. Recapitulation in Like Manner of the Duties Assigned to the Commander of Each Tagma, to the Moirarch, and to the Merarch, So Each May Know What to Look Out For

Whether the bandon or tagma is in service with the rest of the army or is camping someplace by itself, the "Trisagion" must be sung, and the other customary practices observed, early in the morning before any other duty and again in the evening after supper and the dismissal.

The squads, the depth of the files, depending on the quality of the units, should be formed as in the diagram given earlier and should include both old and new men. The first two and the last two men in each file should be armed with the lance, the third and fourth with the bow, and the remainder with whatever they can best handle.

The pennons should not be carried on the lances during combat since they are a bother to the troops carrying them and to those in the rear.

From among the less-qualified soldiers, six or eight should be detailed as corpsmen to take care of the wounded during combat.

Two efficient, alert, and energetic men should be selected as spies or scouts and two as heralds.

Two competent men should be selected as surveyors with the duty of surveying the campsites.

Two soldiers should also be chosen for the quartering parties to reconnoiter the routes.

The two files drawn up next to the standard should be designated to guard it during combat.

A competent orator should be chosen.

One experienced, well-disciplined soldier should be put in charge of guarding the baggage trains.

In the large tagmas two standards should be displayed before the battle, one being that of the commander of the tagma, the other that of the senior hekatontarch, also called ilarch. The young men or files should be divided evenly between them. On the day of battle, however, the two standards should not be raised, but only that of the commanding officer.

On the day of battle, each soldier should carry in his saddlebags a flask of water and a measure or two of biscuit or meal.

Before the end of the battle while the fighting is still going on, no soldier should be allowed to plunder the enemy, and this order should be frequently proclaimed.

The tagma should be formed according to the symbols and diagrams given above.

On the march the soldiers should not get mixed in with the baggage trains, especially if contact with the enemy is expected. Each bandon should march ahead by itself, and the trains to the rear or in such other position as the situation dictates.

Drills should be done according to the movements explained earlier and, if an officer does not know them, details of the nine exercises described should be given him in writing.

It is essential that the horses become accustomed not only to rapid maneuvering in open, level country, but also over hilly, thick, and rough ground, and in quick ascending and descending of slopes. If they get used to these different kinds of terrain, then neither the men nor the horses will be surprised or troubled by any sort of land. Even in hot weather care should be taken not to water the horses too much, and for this reason it is helpful not to camp near rivers. For maneuvers, then, the horses should be brought to difficult country and drilled there, or the bandon should be drawn up in regular formation on rough ground, and each man should gallop over the ground such as he finds it before him and then return the same way. The men who spare their horses and neglect drills of this sort are really planning their own defeat. It is also a good idea for the troops to become used to doing this work in hot weather, for nobody knows what situations may arise.

The end of the seventh book.

· B O O K   V I I I ·
[General Instructions and Maxims]

1. General Instructions for the Commander

(1) In carrying out very critical operations the general ought not set himself apart as though such labor was beneath him, but he should begin the work and toil along with his troops as much as possible. Such behavior will lead the soldier to be more submissive to his officers, even if only out of shame, and he will accomplish more.

(2) When certain offenses are common among the soldiers, moderation is called for. Do not judge and punish all indiscriminately. Widespread resentment might draw them all together, and discipline would become even worse. It is wiser to punish just a few of the ring leaders.

(3) The general's way of life should be plain and simple like that of his soldiers; he should display a fatherly affection toward them; he should give orders in a mild manner; and he should always make sure to give advice and to discuss essential matters with them in person. His concerns ought to be with their safety, their food, and their regular pay. Without these it is impossible to maintain discipline in an army. By being just in punishing offenders he should instill fear. At the very first sign of a disciplinary problem he should take action to end it and not delay dealing with it until it grows more serious. The general is successful when his men regard him as unshakeable and just. He should also see that civilians are left unharmed.

(4) He should be temperate in his way of life and vigilant. It is a good idea to deliberate about difficult problems at night. During the night it is easier to make plans, for one's spirit is free of external disturbance.

(5) It is essential to be cautious and take your time in making

79

plans, and once you come to a decision to carry it out right away without any hesitation or timidity. Timidity after all is not caution, but the invention of wickedness.

(6) A healthy mind is not unduly elated by success nor overly depressed when things are not going well.

(7) It is safer and more advantageous to overcome the enemy by planning and generalship than by sheer force; in the one case the results are achieved without loss to oneself, while in the other some price has to be paid.

(8) It is very important to spread rumors among the enemy that you are planning one thing; then go and do something else. Your plans about major operations should not be made known to many, but to just a few and those very close to you.

(9) One must not always use the same modes of operation against the enemy, even though they seem to be working out successfully. Often enough the enemy will become used to them, adapt to them, and inflict disaster on us.

(10) Alarming rumors of traps or treachery, whether on the part of the enemy or our own, ought not be neglected or action deferred, but steps should be taken to deal with them and put a stop to them before they become realities.

(11) The enemy should be deceived by false reports of our plans brought to them by deserters from us.

(12) Courage should be roused in our troops by fabricating a report of a victory over the enemy won by our men someplace else.

(13) News about reverses suffered by us should be kept secret, and reports stating just the opposite should be circulated about.

(14) Defeated troops should not be allowed to fall into despair, but they should be dealt with by stirring up hope and by various other means.

(15) During combat one has to overlook offenses committed by the soldiers, but afterward get rid of men guilty of sedition.

(16) Our own dead should be buried secretly at night, but the enemy's should be left out there as a means of making them lose courage.

(17) When a delegation comes from the enemy, inquire about the leaders of the group, and on their arrival treat them very friendly, so their own people will come to suspect them.

(18) Acts of cowardice on the part of our soldiers should be kept

quiet and not publicly condemned, since this may make them even worse.

(19) To cross a river unhindered simply dig a deep trench on the riverbank, fill it with wood, have most of the troops cross the river, then the remaining men should set the wood in the trench on fire, and while it is burning they can cross over without trouble.

(20) A way of arousing discord and suspicion among the enemy is to refrain from burning or plundering the estates of certain prominent men on their side and of them alone.

(21) One way of getting a besieged city to submit is by sending letters tied to arrows promising freedom and immunity; this can also be done by releasing prisoners.

(22) Great caution must be observed in pursuing the enemy over ground suited for ambushes. A good general will turn back at the right time, so he can come back later to attack more effectively.

(23) Do not be deceived by humane acts of the enemy or by their pretending to retreat.

(24) Cowardly officers are recognized by their hesitation and pallor; during combat they should be assigned to the auxiliary forces.

(25) When a populous city is taken, it is important to leave the gates open, so that the inhabitants may escape and not be driven to utter desperation. The same holds when an enemy's fortified camp is taken.

(26) Even in friendly territory a fortified camp should be set up; a general should never have to say: "I did not expect it." [1]

(27) For a safe retreat build a fire in one place and quietly go off to another; the enemy will head for the fire.

(28) Letters ought to be sent to deserters from our side who have joined the enemy in such a way that the letters will fall into the enemy's hands. These letters should remind the deserters of the prearranged time for their treachery, so that the enemy will become suspicious of them, and they will have to flee.

(29) When it comes to dangerous or surprise operations, cowards could be weeded out if all men who are sick or whose horses are too weak are ordered to fall out. The cowards will then claim to be

1. This and similar expressions are found in several authors, Polybius, Polyaenus, Cicero, the anonymous On Strategy: see G. Dennis, ed., Das Strategikon des Maurikios, Corpus fontium historiae byzantinae, 17 (Vienna, 1981): 274.

sick, and so they can be separated from the others. They can be assigned to guard fortresses or to some other duty involving little danger.

(30) We should campaign against the enemy when the grain is ripe, so that our troops will not lack provisions and the expedition will cause the enemy more damage.

(31) We should not furnish arms to those who promise to fight on our side because their real intentions are not clear.

(32) After a victory we must not become careless, but be on our guard all the more against surprise attacks by the vanquished.

(33) Envoys from the enemy must not be treated disrespectfully, even when our forces are much stronger.

(34) An army, no matter how strong, besieging a city must never leave its own camp unguarded, nor should it think that fortifications are sufficient to assure its safety, but it should keep sending out patrols.

(35) Suspected defectors should be told the opposite of what we intend to do, so that we may use them to deceive the enemy, and treachery must be guarded against even during periods of truce or temporary peace.

(36) By no means should we believe reports that come from deserters or defectors alone, but their reports should be checked against statements made by prisoners taken in raids, and in this way the truth may be discerned.

(37) In no way should a sworn agreement made with the enemy be broken.

(38) After God, we should place our hopes of safety in our weapons, not in our fortifications alone.

(39) Orders should be given to the soldiers that they should be ready to march out on a holiday, in the rain, day or night. For this reason they should not be told the time or the day beforehand, so they may always be prepared.

(40) Risks should not be taken without necessity or real hope of gain. To do so is the same as fishing with gold as bait.

(41) Inhabitants of the area who seek refuge should not be received indiscriminately. Often enough they have been sent by the enemy deceitfully to plot against their hosts.

(42) We should also be on our guard against deserters who approach a besieged city. Often enough they are sent by the enemy to

set fires so that while the defenders are busy putting them out, the enemy may attack.

(43) Troops defeated in open battle should not be pampered or, even if it seems like a good idea, take refuge in a fortified camp or some other strong place, but while their fear is still fresh, they should attack again. By not indulging them they may with greater assurance renew the fighting.

(44) If the general thinks he is ready to meet the enemy in battle, he should get set to carry on the fighting in the enemy's country instead of his own. Men waging war in a foreign land become more aggressive. They will also feel that the war in which they are engaged is not only being fought on behalf of their country but also their own personal safety. This is not necessarily the case if the war is fought in their own land in which the existence of fortresses eliminates the risks to the men, since in case of flight they may easily take refuge in them.

2. Maxims

(1) Before getting into danger, the general should worship God. When he does get into danger, then, he can with confidence pray to God as a friend.

(2) The man who spends more sleepless nights with his army and who works harder in drilling his troops runs the fewest risks in fighting the foe.

(3) Never lead soldiers into combat before having made sufficient trial of their courage.

(4) It is well to hurt the enemy by deceit, by raids, or by hunger, and never be enticed into a pitched battle, which is a demonstration more of luck than of bravery.

(5) Only those battle plans are successful which the enemy does not suspect before we put them into action.

(6) Deception is often helpful in warfare. An enemy soldier who deserts to us, apart from some plot, is of the greatest advantage, for the enemy is hurt by deserters more than if the same men were killed in action.

(7) He who does not carefully compare his own forces with those of the enemy will come to a disastrous end.

(8) Courage and discipline are able to accomplish more than a

large number of warriors. Often enough the lay of the land has been helpful in making the weaker force come out on top.

(9) Nature produces but few brave men, whereas care and training make efficient soldiers. Soldiers who are kept working improve in courage, while too much leisure makes them weak and lazy. Care should be taken to keep them busy.

(10) Things which are unexpected or sudden frighten the enemy, but they pay little attention to things to which they are accustomed.

(11) After gaining a victory the general who pursues the enemy with a scattered and disorganized army gives away his victory to the foe.

(12) The cause of war must be just.

(13) A good general is one who utilizes his own skills to fit the opportunities he gets and the quality of the enemy.

(14) It does not help to assemble the whole army in council, or to keep sending for men when they are off duty. These things only cause discord in the army.

(15) The soldiers must always be doing something, even if no enemy is bothering us. Habitual idleness spells trouble for an army.

(16) A prudent commander will not lead an allied force into his own country if it is larger than his own army. Otherwise it might mutiny, drive out the native troops, and take over the country.

(17) When possible, an allied force should be composed of various nationalities to reduce the danger of its men uniting for some evil purpose.

(18) We should draw up our forces in the same manner as those of the enemy, infantry against infantry, and so with light-armed troops, cavalry, heavy infantry, and so forth.

(19) The commander who fails to provide his army with necessary food and other supplies is making arrangements for his own defeat, even with no enemy present.

(20) The commander who relies on his own cavalry, especially the lancers, should seek out broad plains favorable to such troops and there force the battle.

(21) If, on the other hand, he relies more on his infantry, he should take care to choose uneven, thick, and rugged terrain for the fighting.

(22) If we hear that our plans have been betrayed to the enemy,

then we ought to change all our passwords and other signals and the shape of our battle formation.

(23) For what should be done seek the advice of many; for what you will actually do take council with only a few trustworthy people; then off by yourself alone decide on the best and most helpful plan to follow, and stick to it.

(24) Either the army must be assembled near its supplies, or those supplies must be transported to it.

(25) Do not rely only on scouts to reconnoiter the roads, but let the general carefully observe them with his own eyes.

(26) Scouts must be chosen who are steady, keen-eyed, reliable, serious, and fonder of their reputation than of money; such men make accurate reports. But those who are light-headed, cowardly, and excited by the prospect of material gain are likely not to tell the truth, and so may easily endanger both the general and his army.

(27) In time of peace, fear and the punishing of offenses keep the troops in line, but on active campaign great expectations and rewards get even better results.

(28) The general achieves the most who tries to destroy the enemy's army more by hunger than by force of arms.

(29) If an enemy spy is captured while observing our forces, then it may be well to release him unharmed if all our forces are strong and in good shape. The enemy will be absolutely dismayed by such reports. On the other hand, if our forces are weak, the spy should be treated roughly, forced to divulge enemy secrets, and finally either be put to death or sent off elsewhere under guard.

(30) If the soldiers show signs of cowardice, various skills should be used to restore their courage.

(31) "Take your time in planning, but when you have made your decision be fast in putting it into action."[2] In war opportunity is fleeting and cannot be put off at all.

(32) Let the army see that you are not unduly elated over successes nor utterly cast down by failures.

(33) It is not the general whose words are frightening but the one who gets things done who is feared by the enemy.

(34) Plan what you have to do at night and carry out your decision during the day. One cannot plan and act at the same time.

2. Isocrates, *Ad Demonicum*, 34.

(35) The general who is overly harsh with his subordinates and the one who is too indulgent are both unfit for command. Fear leads to great hatred, and giving in too much results in being despised. It is best to take the middle course.

(36) After agreeing upon a treaty or a truce with the enemy, the commander should make sure that his camp is guarded more strongly and more closely. If the enemy chooses to break the agreement, they will only gain a reputation for faithlessness and the disfavor of God, while we shall remain in safety and be true to our word. A general should not have to say: "I did not expect it."

(37) For smaller forces we should select a place with a narrow front, whose width corresponds to the size of our army. The superior numbers of the enemy are useless in such a place since there is no room for them. By studying the place where they are, the general can form a fair estimate of the enemy's strength, for he should know from experience how much space is required for a given number of troops.

(38) If we want to keep the enemy from finding out the strength of our forces, we should order them to march on foot and in close formation. This can be deceptive and prevent the enemy from forming a clear estimate of our numbers.

(39) It is a good idea to maneuver so that the sun, wind, and dust are behind our men and in the face of the enemy. By so obscuring his vision and making his breathing difficult, we should quickly be victorious.

(40) We should line up our troops for battle before the enemy gets ready. This puts us in a position to do what we wish, and barely allows the enemy time to arm.

(41) If we are all set for the charge first, then we can attack the enemy in safety with our men full of confidence, and the enemy's very worried.

(42) When the battle line has been drawn up, the first rule is for the soldiers to maintain the formation and the intervals between the lines.

(43) It is right to be very concerned about the wounded. If we neglect them, we will find that the rest of the troops will deliberately not fight well, and our remissness will cause us to lose some who could have been saved.

(44) If the enemy is put to flight, our soldiers must be restrained

from plundering. Otherwise while they are scattered about doing this, the enemy army might reform and attack them.

(45) The general is at fault if most of the army is destroyed in a single battle.

(46) An army which shouts out its war cries good and loud can strike terror into the enemy.

(47) A general who takes nothing for granted is secure in war.

(48) If the enemy has a very strong force of archers, watch for wet weather, which affects the bows, to launch our attack against them.

(49) Our commander ought to adapt his stratagems to the disposition of the enemy general. If the latter is inclined to rashness, he may be enticed into premature and reckless action; if he is on the timid side, he may be struck down by continual surprise raids.

(50) The general should be impartial in dealing with his own men and with allied forces. He should be a just judge for both. When he gives presents to the allies, he should make a regular increase in the gratuities for his own soldiers.

(51) In wartime the general should do more than his share of the work and take less than his share of gain. This will enhance his reputation and secure for him the good will of all.

(52) Aware of the uncertainties of war,[3] the general ought to be ready, even after victory, to listen to proposals of the enemy for peace on advantageous terms.

(53) The general should pay greater attention to arms than to other equipment, aware that other equipment can be obtained even in enemy territory, but that without arms we will not overcome the enemy.

(54) The best general is not the man of noble family, but the man who can take pride in his own deeds.

(55) The general must correctly manage not only matters of immediate concern, but must also take thought for the future.

(56) The best leader is one who does not willingly engage in a hazardous and highly uncertain battle and refrains from emulating those who carry out operations recklessly and are admired for their brilliant success, but one who, while keeping the enemy on the

---

3. The manuscripts have: "The uncertain character of the enemy." Correcting *polemion* to *polemon*, as here translated, may make better sense.

move, remains secure and always in circumstances of his own choosing.

(57) An avaricious general can be the ruin of his own people and an object of contempt to the enemy.

(58) A general who loves luxury can destroy the whole army.

(59) The best commander is the one who can instill courage at the right time and can hold back the headlong flight of frightened soldiers.

(60) A general who desires peace must be prepared for war, for the barbarians become very nervous when they face an adversary all set to fight.

(61) Mistakes made in ordinary affairs can generally be remedied in a short while, but errors made in war cause lasting harm.

(62) Those whose performance is consistently poor should not be entrusted even with just ordinary responsibilities.

(63) The sharp general takes into account not only probable dangers, but also those which may be totally unexpected.

(64) Make peace a time of training for war, and battle an exhibition of bravery.

(65) The general should not go to sleep before reflecting on what he should have done that he might have neglected and on what he has to do the next day.

(66) It is well for the general to exercise self-control at all times, but especially during war.

(67) The general should not be hasty in placing confidence in people who promise to do something; if he does, almost everyone will think he is light headed.

(68) Long and careful deliberation promises great safety in war, whereas hasty and impetuous generals usually commit serious blunders.

(69) The general should set an example of how things ought to be done for his subordinates, training himself in the highest ideals, doing what is right and refraining from those things his soldiers should refrain from.

(70) The general should make sure of the good disposition of his troops by an oath.

(71) If the general knows the inclinations and tendencies of each officer and soldier, he will know better what duties should be assigned to each one.

(72) The general who wants to keep his plans concealed from the

enemy should never take the rank and file of his own troops into his confidence.

(73) When both sides are equally well armed, the better tactician will win.

(74) The general who possesses some skill in public speaking is able, as in the past, to rouse the weak-hearted to battle and restore courage to a defeated army.

(75) The general should know the country well, whether it is healthy and safe or unhealthy for his troops and inhospitable, and whether the necessities such as water, wood, and forage are nearby. For if these are at a distance, then their procurement is difficult and dangerous, especially in the presence of the enemy. It is also good to occupy any hills in the area before the enemy has a chance to do so.

(76) As in the past, misleading moves taken by the general can be very advantageous. For example, if he makes it look as though he is going to set up camp, the enemy may be lured into doing the same thing; then while they are scattered about getting things ready, he may secretly draw up his troops and attack, or he may quietly withdraw his army if the terrain is unfavorable.

(77) In his movements the general should act like a good wrestler; he should feint in one direction to try to deceive his adversary and then make good use of the opportunities he finds, and in this way he will overpower the enemy.

(78) In battles and in every action against the enemy the wise general, even the most courageous, will keep in mind the possibility of failure and defeat and will plan for them as actually occurring.

(79) The spirit of the commander is naturally communicated to the troops, and there is an ancient saying that it is better to have an army of deer commanded by a lion than an army of lions commanded by a deer.[4]

(80) Allied forces should not be mixed in with our own troops. They should set up camp and march separately. It is most important that we hide our formations and methods of warfare from them, for if they ever turn against us, they may use their knowledge of these to hurt us.

(81) In time of war the best way of finding what is advantageous is this: what is advantageous to you is disadvantageous to the enemy, and what is beneficial for them will be just the opposite for your

4. Also cited by Leo, *Tactical Constitutions*, 20, 128.

troops. It is in our interest to do nothing or avoid nothing that the enemy would do or avoid. There is only one thing we should do: whatever we think will be to our advantage. If you imitate the enemy and do what he is doing for his own benefit, you only harm yourself. Conversely, if you do something which is to your advantage, in trying to imitate you the enemy will injure himself.

(82) The troops should be drawn up in several lines, and a number of charges made against the enemy, recalling the words of the poet: "You who are not tired could easily drive men weary with battle back toward the city."[5]

(83) For many reasons, and serious ones at that, it is dangerous to extend the battle line indefinitely.

(84) An army of equal strength is necessary if our aim is merely to defeat the enemy, but it has to be larger if we intend to occupy the conquered territory.

(85) The general would be well advised to have more cavalry than infantry. The latter is set only for close combat, while the former is easily able to pursue or to retreat, and when dismounted the men are all set to fight on foot.

(86) A wise commander will not engage the enemy in a pitched battle unless a truly exceptional opportunity or advantage presents itself.

(87) Change your appearance often so that you look different while forming the battle line, before the charge, in meeting with the enemy, when eating and when sleeping. By so doing you will not be easily captured by the enemy or by some conspirators. Hannibal the Carthaginian used wigs and varied styles of beards, so that the barbarians thought he was a supernatural being.[6]

(88) We should choose the terrain not only to suit our armament, but also with a view to the various peoples. Parthians and Gauls handle themselves well on the plains. The Spanish and Ligurians fight better in the mountains and the hills, and the Britons in the woods, while the Germans are more at home in the swamps.[7]

(89) Whatever terrain the general chooses, he should make his troops familiar with it. They will then be able to avoid rough spots and because of their knowledge of the area will fight the enemy with confidence.

5. Homer, *Iliad*, 11, 802–803; 16, 44–45.
6. Cf. Polybius, *Hist.*, 3, 78, 1–4; Livy, 22, 1.
7. I have not found the source of this.

(90) When the general leads his men out to battle, he should present a cheerful appearance, avoiding any gloomy look. Soldiers usually estimate their prospects by the appearance of the general.

(91) After a victory the general should not allow the men to break ranks right away. For it has happened often enough that the enemy, on noticing that our men have let down their guard in their rejoicing and have broken ranks, have regained their courage, come back to fight and turned our victory into defeat.

(92) When the enemy is surrounded, it is well to leave a gap in our lines to give them an opportunity to flee, in case they judge that flight is better than remaining and taking their chances in battle.

(93) An army is judged by the spirit of its general. Hannibal the Carthaginian understood this well, for when he learned that Scipio was commanding the Romans, he spoke highly of the disposition of their army. Some then criticized him for being so slow to march out and fight against those whom he had often defeated. He defended himself by saying: "I would prefer to deal with a troop of lions commanded by a deer than with a herd of deer under the leadership of a lion."[8]

(94) The state benefits more from a lucky general than from a brave one. The first achieves his results with little effort, whereas the other does so at some risk.

(95) It is better to avoid a tricky opponent than one who never lets up. The latter makes no secret of what he is doing, whereas it is difficult to find out what the other is up to.

(96) The commander should be severe and thorough in investigating charges against his men, but merciful in punishing them. This will gain him their good will.

(97) The general should be calm in emergencies, prudent in counsel, courteous to his associates. He will be most successful in battle if he charges against the enemy, not like a wild beast, but in a calculated manner.

(98) The general should be ignorant of none of the situations likely to occur in war. Who can attempt to accomplish what he does not understand? Who is able to furnish assistance in situations whose dangers he does not understand?

(99) The general must make plans to defeat the enemy not only

8. The same expression is used by Ouranos: J. A. de Foucault, "Douze chapitres inédits de la Tactique de Nicéphore Ouranos," *Travaux et Mémoires* 5 (1973): 311. Its source remains unknown.

by arms but also through their food and drink, making the water unfit to drink and poisoning the grain. He must also know how we can protect ourselves against such measures and how we can avoid falling victim to them.

(100) The general should always have a body of chosen troops about him, whom he can send to the support of sections of the army which are hard pressed. He should not advance too precipitously against the enemy, for if some mishap occurs, the whole army could be destroyed.

(101) When the general gives a public speech he ought also to say something in praise of the enemy. This will convince our men, even when you are praising others, that you will never deprive us of the praise we might receive from others and adorn them with our honors.

· B O O K   I X ·
Surprise Attacks

1. Surprise Attacks

It is of course an ancient maxim that teaches us to try to assault the enemy without ourselves suffering any injury, and intelligent generals will keep this in mind and always give it high priority. This goal can be attained if the assaults on the enemy are carefully planned and swiftly carried out. These assaults can be shown to be very effective not only against forces of equal strength, but also against vastly superior ones. For this reason it is wise to be always on the watch for the right opportunities and pretexts and to strike at the enemy before they can get themselves ready, especially if there is reason to believe that their forces are stronger than ours. In such cases it is better, as has been said, to try to employ different surprises and tricks as much as possible rather than engage in a pitched battle which involves dangers which could prove fatal.

Some commanders have welcomed embassies from the enemy and replied in gentle and flattering terms, sent them on their way with honors, and then immediately followed along and attacked them unexpectedly. Some have themselves sent embassies with favorable proposals and then suddenly launched an attack. Some have gone after the enemy in their camps by getting information about how securely they set up camp, and then on a moonlit night two or three hours before daybreak they would make their attack. Archers are essential for an operation of this sort. On learning that the enemy was marching along in disorder and allowing their troops to straggle, some commanders have attacked them in the middle of their march and inflicted serious injury. Others hiding in ambush have suddenly charged out to attack the enemy. Some have pretended to withdraw from the scene of the action, then wheeled around all of a sudden and charged into the enemy. Some others have driven herds of animals ahead of them, so the enemy would turn aside to round them up and then, when they saw the enemy disordered and scattered about, they would fall upon them.

Some attacks can be made out in the open, for example, if there is a river in the area between us and the enemy which is difficult to cross, especially for cavalry. A bridge can be constructed there, either with wooden crossbeams as most of them are usually built, or on pontoons, and with towers erected at both ends, either of wood, dry masonry, or earth. When necessary, then, this bridge may be used to cross over safely or to withdraw, and it leaves it up to the general to decide how long to remain in that place, whether to attack in safety or to retreat and destroy the bridge. In operations of this sort, however, and in incursions into the enemy's territory we ought not burn or destroy supplies in those regions through which we hope to return, or our own men will suffer. We think it essential to have such bridges also in case of a pitched battle when the camps are set up close to a river. If crossing proves to be difficult at any point along the river bank, especially in the area where the enemy are stationed, on the day of battle the army may still be led out without hindrance and without crowding. In case of a reverse they can remain safely in the protection of the camp, and they will not be forced against their will to cross the bridge under hostile fire. For these reasons the camp should be set up on the enemy's side of the river.

2. Attacks at Night

The conduct of night attacks has varied among commanders. Some have pitched camp about a day's march from the enemy, and have sent a deputation or two to offer proposals for peace. When the enemy have reason to hope that an agreement is being reached, and they become careless, then these generals march their army at night and attack unexpectedly before dawn. This was done by the Roman general Lusius in the time of Trajan.[1] Others have drawn up in combat formation for several days near their own camp as if for a pitched

1. Lusius is mentioned by Dio Cassius in several places, as well as by other authors. The incident here reported apparently took place near Nisibis or Edessa in A.D. 116: Pauly-Wissowa, *Realenzyklopädie der classischen Altertumswissenschaft* (Stuttgart, 1893ff.), 2, 13, 1874–90.

battle. They pretended to be frightened by the enemy and on this account would not stray beyond the area of their own camp. Then, while the enemy were relaxing, they would attack them at night. This is what the khan of the Avars did to the Roman cavalry at Heracleia, for it did not stay safely inside the fortifications with the infantry, but was outside unprotected.[2] Still others would make use of a pretended deserter to inform the enemy that the morale of the army was low. They would then simulate a withdrawal far to the rear, but would go only a short distance and there set up their encampment. Then suddenly at night they would attack the enemy.

Night attacks are best made by archers or javelin throwers, both mounted and dismounted. They are effective against peoples, whether on foot or on horseback, who do not fortify or set up their camps properly but pitch their tents all over the place and without protection. They are also effective against peoples who are not skilled in using the bow and javelin, but prefer to engage in hand-to-hand fighting. These operations should be carried out on nights when there is enough light, either from the moon or the stars, along the whole line of march to keep the men from bumping into one another in the darkness or getting lost. The army should always move on the alert and ready for action, carrying only what is necessary. They should regulate their march according to the distance between the two camps so as to arrive two hours before dawn someplace about one or two miles from the enemy's camp, marching easily so they will not be exhausted. There the army should stay in hiding and rest, and then attack the enemy just before dawn.

Expeditions of this sort must be guided by men who know the country very thoroughly and who will not lead the army astray. Absolute silence must be observed, no bugle calls or other loud noises of any kind. If, however, it should be necessary for the army to halt or to advance, the signal may be given by a whistle, a simple striking on a shield, or by a command. To avoid any noisy confusion or stretching the formation out too much, resulting in straggling, an uneven line, the shouting of commands, all of which clearly betray the approach of the army to the enemy, it must move, not by the front as for battle, but in column, that is, in a straight line, the units marching in a file one behind the other, observing of course the depth of the

2. In A.D. 592: Theophylact of Simocatta, *History*, 6, 5; H. Mihăescu, "Prolégomènes à une édition critique des Taktika-Strategika de Maurice-Urbicius," *Revue des études sud-est européennes* 5 (1967): 401–17.

formation. When the army gets close to the enemy, then they should rest under cover, straighten out their line and, depending on the terrain, launch their attack from two or three sides. It should not be made from all four sides, for then the enemy finding themselves completely surrounded will be forced to close ranks and fight, but one side should be left open so those who want to flee may do so. At that time, if the attacking army is large, one or two trumpets should be blown; if it is small more should be blown to make them think it is larger.

Some units of the army should always be held in reserve, taking no part in the action at that time, but standing by until needed to provide cover for their own men who might be fleeing. Attacks of this sort, especially if against cavalry, must be made very carefully and with a good deal of preparation, just as for a pitched battle. Then, if it should not proceed according to plan, but the enemy has been warned and lines up in formation to meet us, our army may find itself unprepared and be routed in the ensuing battle. If the opposing force consists of infantry, and our attack is made with cavalry, then it is obvious that they will cause serious harm to the enemy, or they themselves will be able to retire without injury, for the infantry will not be able to pursue them. Whether the attack is made at night against a fortified camp or in the daytime or against troops on the march or against their baggage train, certain units must be clearly designated to seize supplies and such. Otherwise, if all or most of the soldiers become engaged in this, the enemy might attack and endanger the whole army.

3. Incursions into Hostile Territory; Security While on the March in It; Plundering It Without Suffering Damage

One can safely attempt an incursion into hostile territory under two conditions: if the assault is made after the enemy has been defeated in battle or if we know that they are unprepared or unfit for action should they be attacked without warning. This is true even if the enemy forces are more numerous, and certainly if they are undisciplined and disorganized, such as the Slavs, Antes, and other undisciplined, disorganized peoples. Or our men can seize and hold a position, such as a riverbank or mountain pass, from which they can hurt the enemy without being touched by them.

Above all, the general must be concerned about the supplies for the army when it enters enemy territory. He must see that these are transported in common baggage wagons, by the individual soldier, or in some other way. For if the enemy should destroy the local provisions, the army might suddenly find itself in critical straits in the middle of a hostile land. Marches should generally not be made at night in hostile territory, unless, of course, it is done to maintain secrecy. For example, it may be absolutely necessary to avoid detection by the enemy, to seize difficult ground quickly or to pass over it without the enemy finding out. But before setting out on any such march, great care must taken to reconnoiter the roads.

Serious efforts should be made to capture inhabitants of the country alive in order to obtain information from them about the strength and the plans of the enemy. Interrogation of prisoners should be done by the general in person and not by someone else. Frequently very important and completely unsuspected information has been revealed by such questioning. Do not, however, put much trust in statements of deserters or defectors, certainly not as much as in men captured in surprise attacks. For it is not uncommon for deserters and captives to give false information deliberately. Do not pay attention to statements made by one person, and do not believe anything unless it is corroborated by several others, especially, as mentioned, in the case of prisoners taken in raids or deserters. Deserters from the enemy who claim to have some secret information should be placed in confinement or securely held in some other way and told that if their statements prove true they will be rewarded but if false they will be put to death.

If the enemy army is concentrated someplace outside their fortifications, none of our soldiers should be allowed to go off to plunder and loot, but they should first advance against the enemy. If the result of the battle is favorable, they should not put off the opportunity but, while the enemy is still very frightened and confused, they should keep after them until their forces are completely broken up and scattered or until favorable peace terms with unequivocal guarantees are made. If the enemy is indeed concentrated but avoids getting into action, then our troops, while remaining united, must ride about and trample everything under foot. But if we plan on returning by the same route and are not well provided with food or forage, then we should spare the local supplies and destroy them only on our return journey. The vanguard should place some signs at forks in the road and other places where mistakes can be made. If it is a wooded area, they can be put on the trees; if barren, piles of rocks or mounds of earth will do. These will be recognized by the troops marching along behind, and the army will not get lost.

Troops sent out to pillage should not all be involved in the plundering, but divided into two groups, the first to do the pillaging and the other more numerous group to follow along to guard them. This should be observed whether the expedition is directed against a region, a fortified enemy camp, a herd of cattle, a baggage train, or anything else. The same procedure should be followed if the whole army joins together in a pillaging expedition. All the men should not engage in pillaging, but if the opportunity for collecting supplies presents itself, some should go out gathering them, and others should follow along in regular formation. If all the soldiers are busy with plundering and collecting provisions, they might be caught by a surprise attack or an ambush before they can get themselves back in formation.

Except in an emergency, we think it is more advantageous not to pick a few men from different units and detail them for an expedition, a scouting party, or some other military duty. It is better to detail an entire tagma or bandon or one of their subdivisions under an ilarch or dekarch. It may become necessary to form a special detail in certain circumstances, for example, if most of the soldiers are reluctant for whatever reason to do the job or if the horses are in poor condition. In such circumstances, then, the detail should be composed of men whose morale is high and whose horses are in good condition. In general, though, taking a few men at random from each tagma for some duty is dangerous. The men so detailed cannot be used to the best advantage since they miss the support of their friends and they do not know one another. Furthermore, the units left behind are deprived of their best soldiers.

When the general plans to seize a fortress or height or some other place, he should not let his men know about it until they are actually on the site and he orders them to begin the task. If it is really necessary for the army to encamp or to pass close by a fortified position of the enemy, one of the officers with some light armed troops should be stationed near the entrance ways of the fortification to prevent any sudden sally by the enemy. The same precautions should be taken in passing through defiles. A bivouac or camp should not be set up in the vicinity of an enemy fortification or a wooded area. But if it is absolutely necessary to camp there, careful attention should be given to the guardposts in case of enemy attacks at night. It is better to look for open, unobstructed, high, and defensible ground for camping.

On entering hostile territory the baggage train should follow behind, but on getting closer to the enemy, it should take up position in the middle of the army. The trains and the prisoners, if there are any, should be kept separated from the regular troops, both on the march and in camp, so they will not get in the way of the soldiers if they have to fight off a sudden enemy attack. In enemy country, surveyors or quartering parties should not be sent out ahead without due precaution and sufficient support. It is safe enough to rely on prisoners and deserters for information about the nature of the ground.

In making camp the army should march into the enclosure in proper formation and good order. But, if the enemy come near, and there are infantry in the army, first park the wagons, then dig the trench in the prescribed way, station all the light-armed troops ready for action a short distance away. The baggage train should then enter in good order and encamp. The outposts can then be withdrawn, and the soldiers themselves enter in formation and set up camp. But if the enemy is not in the vicinity, it is sufficient to follow this procedure with a single droungos or meros, and all the rest go and pitch camp.

If the enemy is nearby and in close formation, or if our camp is near a wooded area or rough ground, do not let the horses out to graze freely, but keep them inside the camp and be sure to send out scouting parties. Take care to collect provisions either from what is found in nearby villages or organize the boys to gather forage, but make sure they are accompanied by light-armed troops from each meros proceeding in formation in case of sudden enemy attacks. If the army spends some time in the place, and if there is opportunity and room for foraging, assuming that the enemy forces are a good distance away, then the horses may be allowed to graze. But double, even triple, patrols should be systematically sent out in all directions to a considerable distance and relieved at regular intervals. Any soldiers who on their own authority join parties duly and officially assigned to plundering should be detained and sent to their own commanders for punishment. If everyone takes leave to go out pillaging, the general will find himself without any troops, and the whole army will be endangered.

Any wine or grain found locally should not be drunk or eaten before it has been tested by giving it to prisoners. Water from the wells should not be drunk for it will often have been poisoned. We ourselves recall that in the Persian wars even the barley was spoiled by some poison, and a number of horses perished.[3] Since there was no fodder about, the soldiers were forced to give the local barley to their horses.

Instructions should be given to the men that in the event of an unexpected disturbance while on the march, they should not race about and get in each other's way, but everyone should hurry to that section in which the disturbance occurs. By following this procedure they will be prepared for the enemy, better able to concentrate their forces and to avoid confusion. Not only should effective patrols always be maintained to the front in case of attack, but a fairly strong force, well armed but without much equipment, called a rear guard, under a competent officer, should be stationed about fifteen or twenty miles to the rear. It should set up good patrols in case there are stragglers from the army who fall behind because of illness or some other reason, or in case of sudden enemy attacks. The best time for such attacks is when the troops are marching along carelessly and when those up ahead cannot easily come to the support of the troops behind them. It is not a bad idea to do this even in our own country to deal with soldiers wandering about without permission of their commanders and acting disorderly, and to identify men disregarding their military obligations.

4. The Passage of Defiles and Difficult Country

Apart from a serious emergency, we do not recommend that cavalry, while in hostile territory, march through long stretches of thick and rugged country, a feat difficult enough for infantry; this would be particularly imprudent during the summer. Even though such defiles are difficult for foot soldiers, still, if they are only a mile or so long, the cavalry can dismount and hike through them safely. We define as difficult those defiles which have only one passable road. When other routes exist or can be improvised, the defile may be passed without hindrance.

Now, if our army does have to pass through narrow defiles, and

3. *Chronique de Jean évêque de Nikiou*, ed. and trans. H. Zotenberg (Paris 1883), c. 96, p. 408.

we hope to return by the same route, and if it is wooded and, as just described, not very long, then when we first go through it trees should be cut down, and the ground leveled and cleared in the regular fashion. If the way is narrow and precipitous, so that it cannot be leveled, then a detachment of sufficient strength, either of horse or foot, should be sent ahead to seize it and to take up position on commanding points until we return. In more critical locations it may be necessary to do both, cut down the trees or clear the ground and leave a suitable guard. Troops passing through the defile, accompanied by supply trains or plunder, should divide into two groups or formations marching on foot in column by the flank, especially when they are carrying plunder. They should do this even if they are infantry, who can usually pass through thick, rugged, or narrow areas with ease. If the army consists only of cavalry, the troops should dismount and place the baggage and equipment in the center. In such situations and places, in addition to the double column assigned to guard the baggage and plunder they might have, a strong force of good, light-armed troops must be chosen from the main body, stationed on the four sides of the double column as the terrain permits. Their task is to march alongside and ward off any hostile parties trying to harass the column. This should allow the main body to protect the baggage and plunder without being split up or disordered, or its men drawn off to fight attackers. For how can the troops in the double column do everything, protect the plunder properly and deal with hostile raiding parties? For this reason, then, the troops who can be spared must be assigned to march outside the double column on all four sides, especially to the rear. In this manner it is relatively easy to pass through the most difficult places under any conditions. If there are no infantry in the force, and the cavalry, therefore, dismounts and proceeds on foot, their horses should not be left with them but led along in the center. Otherwise, if the men marching along become alarmed or disturbed, even without reason, and their horses are close by, they can easily mount them, break ranks, and cause serious harm. If the column includes prisoners or plunder, and if the enemy appears on one side of the line of march or both, the prisoners, still bound, should be lined up outside of the column and used as a shield. Either the enemy will hold their fire out of consideration for them, or if they do shoot, they will kill the prisoners instead of our soldiers. If on marching out the army runs into an unexpected critical situation, and gets bogged down in the narrow

passes, and cannot withdraw without real danger, then it is better to
come to an agreement with the enemy, relinquishing a part or all of
the plunder. Thus the army can extricate itself safely instead of
taking unnecessary risks. But if they do not want to make such an
agreement, then the prisoners should be put to death before the eyes
of the enemy. The army may then either remain in that country and
ravage it without mercy or, as best they can, maintain formation and
concentrate on escape. The major concern of the general who is
caught in such a defile, especially a long one, should be not to try to
force his way through, particularly in summer when the dense foliage enables the enemy to cause more trouble, before all enemy
forces have been driven off, or his own troops have seized the commanding heights of the passage.

5. Spying on the Enemy. The Capture of Scouts or Spies Trying to Hide in Our Army

The arrangement of cavalry and infantry formations and the disposition of other units cause great differences in their apparent strength.
An inexperienced person casually looking at them may be very far off
in his estimates. Assume a cavalry formation of six hundred men
across and five hundred deep, which comes to three hundred thousand troops. Each horse in the formation occupies a space three feet
wide, the whole line then being eighteen hundred feet, and each
space is eight feet long, so that the entire line is four thousand feet
deep. The rectangle thus formed by the two sides along the width,
each of eighteen hundred feet, and the two sides of the depth, the
four thousand feet, all told add up to eleven thousand six hundred
feet, making the perimeter of the rectangle two and a quarter miles,
and containing three hundred thousand soldiers. But now if we line
them up in a single long line, allowing a space three feet wide for
each horse, this comes to nine hundred thousand feet, which equals
one hundred and eighty miles. If they march in scattered groups, we
must admit that they will occupy a much greater space and to the
observer will appear more numerous than if they were in regular
formation. All the more so if they are marching on sloping or hilly
ground.

Hence, if a commander wants to make his army appear more formidable, he can form it in a very thin line, extend it a long distance,
or leave gaps in the line. An observer would not be able to estimate

its fighting strength or anything else. And in this connection, there are other points to be considered. If the army is well equipped and the men and horses present a good appearance, instead of keeping them close together, form lines of thin, uneven depth not very far apart. If it simply appears large, spread the troops out over the area and have them camp in different places. Since, therefore, there are such great differences in formations and organization, scouting must not be entrusted to inexperienced men or complete confidence placed in their reports. Most people are incapable of forming a good estimate if an army numbers more than twenty or thirty thousand, especially if they are Scythians, who are mostly horsemen. Then too, one should not be easily troubled and imagine a huge army when he observes a long, thin battle line. Unless its depth is proportionate, its actual strength will not be great. The depth should be investigated. Is the baggage train drawn up behind the main force or does it consist only of fighting men? More accurate information about an army's numerical strength may be obtained from deserters, from prisoners, from the passage of narrow defiles, from camps when all the enemy forces make camp together.

When a camp is not fortified, outposts should be set up depending on the nature of the terrain. If the approaches are narrow, a few will suffice. In unobstructed and open country, there should be more of them, in different places, in touch with one another, and further out. Vigilance is particularly necessary at night when the enemy can easily and freely move in to observe the outposts, and if they are weak, they can sneak up and surprise them. For this reason the outposts should be at a distance from one another and frequently change location.

It is the duty of scouts, who should be intelligent and alert, to observe closely the positions and movements of the enemy. The men chosen for this should be lightly armed and mounted on fast horses. Spies should be very bold and move right in among the enemy, so they may be regarded as belonging to the same race. The men making up the patrols should be reliable; they should look very manly and be a cut above the other soldiers in physical appearance, morale, and equipment, so they may project a noble image in confronting the enemy and if captured, make a good impression on them. The officer in charge of the patrol should be well above average, selected for his alertness, intelligence, and experience. For this sort of assignment requires intelligence and alertness more than bravery. While the enemy is still reported to be far off, only the scouts should be sent out when the general wants to gather information about the enemy's movements, the nature of the roads, or fortified places. When a raid is planned for the purpose of taking prisoners, the scouts should join up with the patrols, but should go ahead of them to observe from concealed positions, and the patrols should follow along the route they indicate.

In hazardous circumstances more than one patrol should be sent out and in more than one direction. They should vary and be constantly changing according to the nature of the ground. They should be far enough apart so that if the enemy stays at a good distance from our men and manages to elude one of the patrols, they will run into others and be discovered. The most advanced patrol need not consist of many men. The next one in should have more, and the third still more. The patrols must be inspected to see how they are doing. Very reliable officers should be sent to make unexpected visits to observe how things are going. Anyone found negligent should be punished for seriously endangering the whole army. An experienced scout, even before the enemy comes in view, should be able to estimate the strength of their army from certain signs, such as the extent of ground trampled by their horses and the size of their camp. He should be able to estimate the time when they passed through the area from the droppings of men and horses and from their tracks.

If the camp is fortified by a ditch or a regular stone wall and the mounted troops have been allowed to go inside the fortifications, then the patrols should not be sent too far off to avoid unnecessarily wearing out the horses. But if the cavalry is bivouacked outside, the patrols should be carefully organized.

Soldiers sent out on patrol duty should be instructed to take prisoners. They should be trained for this just as for hunting, stalking them unseen and undetected. A few should show themselves and then draw back while others circle around as unseen and concealed as the ground allows. Individuals should show themselves in several places while the main body heads for another place where they can hide themselves through the night. The best time for this is when the enemy is reported to be far off and would not suspect such activity. Patrol assignments should be kept secret not only from the enemy, but also from the rank and file of our army. If this is observed, soldiers who want to desert will unexpectedly fall right into their hands.

The commanding officers of the tagmas should be entrusted with the responsibility for capturing spies or scouts. Each officer should announce to his men that on the next day about the second or third hour a trumpet will sound. Everyone, soldier or servant, must immediately go into his own tent. Anyone who dares to be found outside the tents will be punished. After everyone has gone inside, then, the officers themselves should stay outside, observe, and arrest anyone found standing around outside the tents. The squad members should hold any stranger entering the tent and hand him over to their own commander. One of two things will result: the arrest of a stranger standing outside because he will not know where to go, or he may be bold enough to enter the tent of one of the squads, will be recognized as a foreigner and handed over to the commander. Everyone caught in this manner must be detained, whether they appear to be Romans or foreigners, and they should be interrogated to find out their true status. This may be done easily in a regular camp in which the army, cavalry or infantry is concentrated, or it may be done separately in camps of a single meros or tagma. Spies may also be detected by other means and a variety of such signals; different orders or signals may be given which require some definite action. These procedures not only expose enemy spies, but they also accustom our own soldiers to obey their officers and to follow orders carefully, particularly if a reasonable punishment is given to those who are careless in these matters. It is not a bad idea to issue other orders of this nature, especially when the troops are at leisure, to test them and to get them used to following orders.

· B O O K   X ·
[Sieges]

1. Laying Siege to the Enemy's Fortresses if the Opportunity Arises

Our camp must be very strongly fortified, and a large number of our sharpest scouts should be stationed around, covering even the most unlikely places, in order to prevent the besieged or forces outside the walls from suddenly attacking us, either by day or by night, and exposing the army to danger. This is what happened in Arzanene when some of our commanders were captured while besieging a fortress.[1]

The first thing the besieger should do, if possible, is to keep the necessities, such as food and water, from getting to the people within the walls. If the besieged possess these supplies in abundance, then it is necessary to resort to siege engines and fighting. Try to have soldiers who present a handsome physical appearance and whose horses are nicely equipped get as close to the enemy fortifications as they can safely do and let the besieged get a good look at them. Keep the less-impressive troops farther off with the supplies, far enough distant so that the people within the walls cannot come to any judgment about the men or the animals, but will think they are all men and of the same quality as those they had seen earlier by the walls. It is also a good idea to get the besieged to believe that we have a large number of armed men; to do this make the men who do not have coats of mail wear the mail hoods of those who do, so that from a distance it will look as though they too are wearing mail. We should set up our camp far enough away to get them to believe that all the objects they see in it are really soldiers.

In the beginning you should not offer terms which are severe and

---

1. This probably refers to the Roman siege of the fortress of Aqbas in Arzanene, a region of Armenia, in 583: Theophylact of Simocatta, *History*, 1, 12.

harsh to the besieged. If the terms are too severe the defenders may think that the risk of fighting is the lesser of two evils and may become desperate and united. But try to make terms lighter and more acceptable, such as the surrender of their horses, weapons, or some other possessions. Such a moderate approach with its hopes of safety may lead them to differences of opinion, and they may become more hesitant to resist and face danger. In case of a lengthy siege make sure all your supplies are arranged for ahead of time. Estimate the number of men required for each duty and type of work, and be sure to assign each man to his task.

The whole army must not be brought out every day to assault the walls. This would leave them all exhausted at once. Rather, the army should be divided into various sections and a certain number of troops assigned to work so many hours each day. Some should be scheduled to work at night, others during the day. For not only must the besieged be harassed by constant attacks during the day, but they should be kept on edge all night by troops designated for this purpose. In order that the soldiers in our army should not be bothered and disturbed by the shouts of men or the clash of arms, the camp should be pitched a mile or two from the enemy fortifications, beyond earshot of the noise and confusion of the siege. Assaults should not be made recklessly and without purpose. Some losses will occur which will only discourage our troops and encourage the besieged. If the besieged fort is small and a direct assault appears risky and costly, and the besieged are well supplied, then work at harassing them constantly, night and day, until they are exhausted. If there are houses of inflammable material within the walls, fire-bearing arrows should be shot from various directions, especially if there is a strong wind blowing. Also catapults should be used to hurl the so-called incendiary bombs. While the enemy is kept busy trying to extinguish the fires, set up ladders, if the ground permits, and climb up. In almost all sieges catapults are useful, especially if it is difficult to get close by digging or piling up earth or to get a battering ram in position.

2. Meeting Hostile Incursions into Our Own Country

If an enemy force, superior in strength or even equal to ours, invades our country, especially at the beginning of the invasion, we must be sure not to engage it in pitched battle. We should, instead, carefully lay ambushes by day or by night, block the route it is taking, seize strong points beforehand, destroy supplies along its line of march. If there is to be an attack, it is more effective to make it as the enemy is returning and leaving our country, when they are encumbered with plunder, tired out, and getting closer to their own people. If you do want to engage them in battle, that is the time to attack. For a person operating in his own country is less inclined to fight; he has many ways of saving himself and does not want to take unnecessary risks. One marching through enemy country, on the other hand, would out of desperation prefer fighting and would regard any retreat as hazardous.

It is most important to keep the army unharmed and intact. By concentrating on this, the enemy will not find it easy to besiege the fortifications or disperse his forces to ravage the country, for he will be under observation and will have to reckon with a concentrated army.

Even though the general decides against a pitched battle, he should still make preparations for one. He should make it appear that he plans on one and convey the impression to all his troops that he will definitely attack the enemy. This will cause trouble for the enemy when it comes to their knowledge.

If the nature of the ground and the situation of the enemy's country are favorable, make plans to send a force there by another route as a diversionary tactic. Of course, as already noted, it is necessary to study the situation and the distances, so that if the enemy learns of the raid and moves against our force, they can safely leave the country by another route and avoid being trapped there by the enemy movement.

All essential supplies must be collected in very strong fortresses, and the country should be cleared of animals. If the enemy should lay siege to one of our fortified places, we should destroy provisions in the vicinity and ambush men sent out to gather supplies, and so make it very tight for the enemy.

Forts which are not in a strong natural setting should be made more secure. Part of the army, depending on the progress of the fighting, should be assigned to their defense. Preparations should be made to transfer the inhabitants of weaker places to more strongly fortified ones.

3. Withstanding a Siege Expected to Be Lengthy

You should find out how much time the enemy has to spend on a siege and give careful thought to the provisions you will need. If you

are well supplied with the necessary provisions, fine, otherwise before the enemy approaches evacuate all those who will be useless,
such as the women, the elderly, the infirm, and the children, so that
what provisions you have may be reserved for the able fighting men.
Devices to defend against stone-throwing artillery should be pro-
cured. As protection against these, heavy mats can be hung over the
walls along the battlements, or bundles, coils of rope, loose logs.
Brick facing can also be built onto the ramparts. Against battering
rams, cushions or sacks filled with grain husks and sand are effective.
To ward off the swinging or beaked rams, use grappling irons, pitch,
fire, or heavy, sharpened stones held by ropes or chains which can be
suddenly dropped from machines and then hauled up again by other
counterweights.

If they move up siege towers, hurl fire bombs or stones at them. If
this does not stop them, build towers inside the walls opposite them.
It is necessary that the towers of the wall which are most exposed to
attack should be without roofs, so the soldiers stationed there can
fight without any obstacles, and so that artillery can be easily mounted
there and operated. Small, narrow doors should be cut into these
towers opening to the side toward the right of the siege engines
drawn up by the enemy, so that our infantry can go out through
these side doors and attack while safely covered by their shields and
supported by the troops on top of the wall; in this way they will be
able to force the enemy to pull back their equipment. These small
doors should have gates so they can be secured when necessary and
not remain open.

The garrison should be distributed all along the wall, and a suitable force should be taken from the other troops and held in reserve
to support a threatened sector when necessary. In an emergency,
then, the troops defending the wall will not have to dash from place
to place, leaving certain spots wide open, a very dangerous thing to
do. If the civil population stays in the city, they too must join with the
men distributed along the wall to help the soldiers. This keeps them
too busy to plan an uprising, and it also entrusts them with some
responsibility for the defense of the city and makes them ashamed
to rebel.

The gates of the city should be entrusted to reliable men. No soldiers or civilians should be permitted, especially at the beginning of
the siege, to go outside the walls to fight even though the garrison
may be very strong and courageous. Direct contact with the enemy
could be allowed if it becomes necessary to force some siege engine

which is causing severe damage to pull back from the wall. But in general, the defense should be carried on from the top of the wall and not by having men risk their lives outside in hand-to-hand fighting. For when that sort of thing happens, the best soldiers are killed or wounded, and the rest of the troops become so discouraged that they are easily defeated by the enemy. It is obvious that as long as there are enough men the wall will be secure, but if one point is given up, all the rest will be endangered. If the fortification has an outer wall, it is a good idea to post sentries there, especially at night, when some might think of deserting to the enemy or secretly plan treacherous acts against the defense of the wall. Missiles should be thrown from the wall only when they will be effective.

If the supply of drinking water comes from cisterns or from the ground, its use should be restricted to a certain extent. No individual should have the authority to use as much as he wants. The sentries and their reliefs should be carefully scheduled, especially at night. The distribution of provisions must be strictly regulated, and they should be kept safely under guard, so they cannot easily be stolen by anyone passing by.

4. Building a Border Fortress by Stealth and Without Open Battle

Thorough reconnaissance should be used to find a strong site capable of being walled about with dry materials in ten or twelve days and of being defended by a small garrison in the event of an enemy attack. The reconnaissance party should also find out if there is stone, wood, or brick readily available in the vicinity, and if there is water there or if ways can be devised to procure it. A sufficient force of artisans should be organized, gates and machines for the walls gotten ready, and a good-sized supporting force of brave, well-armed infantry under intelligent and courageous officers should be chosen and given provisions for three or four months. If it is summer the crops in the vicinity should be burned, but if this is difficult to do, destroy them in some other way. Spread the rumor that you are going to attack the enemy in some other place and send out a force, due provision being made for security, toward that place, so the enemy may be diverted in that direction. Then on the very next day try to encourage the troops who are to form the garrison there; incite them to do their task by giving them some rewards and by promising others. While the enemy is occupied off in that other place, all of a sudden move the whole army into the original location, set up secure outposts, have the infantry pitch camp around the fortification and dig a deep ditch if the ground permits. If there are stones or bricks in the area, build a dry wall braced securely along its length with logs. If wood is the only available building material, use some of it, but make the fortified area much smaller.

After enclosing the area in this manner, if the enemy move up to attack the place and the general knows he cannot confront them in a pitched battle, he should withdraw before their approach and arrange to camp nearby. In this way he will not be so close to the enemy that he will be forced to do battle, nor too far from the men in the fortification to prevent the enemy from putting excessive pressure on them. Signals should be arranged, some for the day and some for the night, by means of which the garrison may communicate its situation to the force outside, so that they can come to their assistance when necessary. If circumstances are favorable and the infantry is able to drive off the enemy by fighting, they must not delay at all, so as not to endanger the garrison. As soon as the situation becomes more secure, the fortifications should be built up into a regular, solid construction, made stronger with mortar, and all other details organized. Against a people depending largely on horses, an expedition of this sort can best be undertaken about July, August, or September. During those months the grass is dry and burns easily, and the enemy cavalry find it difficult to stay in one place for any length of time.

If the site has no water supply, no streams or wells, then it is necessary to arrange for large earthenware jars or well-built barrels. They should be filled with water and some clean gravel from a riverbed dropped in. Enough water should be stored to last until winter, and until regular cisterns to hold the rainwater are built. To prevent the water stored in the casks from becoming stagnant and fetid, peg holes should be drilled in them and receptacles placed below, so the water may flow into them drop by drop and kept in motion. When the small receptacles are full, they should be emptied back into the jars or barrels. By this constant movement the water is aerated and does not become foul. It helps to pour some vinegar into water which has started to turn bad, for this quickly lessens or gets rid of the odor. Good thick planks can be prepared, placed in a trench, and fastened together like a box. The seams and joints should be sealed with pitch and tow or wicker, and in this way a regular, moderate-sized cistern is prepared. One or more may be built, mea-

111

suring twenty by ten feet wide and eight or ten feet high. These will do until cement cisterns can be built. For it is well known that water keeps better in large containers. Wooden ties should be placed in the middle of the cisterns, and the planks should be thick, so they will not give way because of the water pressure, and the water will not spill out.

· B O O K   X I ·
Characteristics and Tactics
of Various Peoples

INTRODUCTION

Having discussed the principles of organizing and commanding cavalry, without which, so we believe, it is impossible to confront the enemy with any degree of safety, we must now treat of the tactics and characteristics of each race which may cause trouble to our state.[1] The purpose of this chapter is to enable those who intend to wage war against these peoples to prepare themselves properly. For all nations do not fight in a single formation or in the same manner, and one cannot deal with them all in the same way. Some, whose boldness is unlimited, are led by an impulsive spirit, while others use good judgment and order in attacking their enemies.

1. Dealing with the Persians

The Persian nation is wicked, dissembling, and servile, but at the same time patriotic and obedient. The Persians obey their rulers out of fear, and the result is that they are steadfast in enduring hard work and warfare on behalf of their fatherland. For the most part they prefer to achieve their results by planning and generalship; they stress an orderly approach rather than a brave and impulsive one. Since they have been brought up in a hot climate, they easily bear the hardships of heat, thirst, and lack of food. They are formidable when laying siege, but even more formidable when besieged. They are extremely skillful in concealing their injuries and coping bravely with adverse circumstances, even turning them to their own advantage.

1. John Wiita, "The Ethnika in Byzantine Military Treatises" (Ph.D. diss., University of Minnesota, 1977), provides a very detailed commentary on Book XI.

They are intractable in negotiations. They will not initiate any proposal, even one they regard as vitally important for themsélves, but
will wait until the proposal is made by their opponents.

They wear body armor and mail, and are armed with bows and
swords. They are more practiced in rapid, although not powerful
archery, than all other warlike nations. Going to war, they encamp
within fortifications. When the time of battle draws near they surround themselves with a ditch and a sharpened palisade. They do not
leave the baggage train within, but make a ditch for the purpose of
refuge in case of a reverse in battle. They do not allow their horses to
graze, but gather the forage by hand.

They draw up for battle in three equal bodies, center, right, left,
with the center having up to four or five hundred additional picked
troops. The depth of the formation is not uniform, but they try to
draw up the cavalrymen in each company in the first and second line
or phalanx and keep the front of the formation even and dense. The
spare horses and the baggage train are stationed a short distance behind the main line. In fighting against lancers they hasten to form
their battle line in the roughest terrain, and to use their bows, so that
the charges of the lancers against them will be dissipated and broken
up by the rough ground. Before the day of battle a favorite ploy of
theirs is to camp in rugged country and to postpone the fighting,
especially when they know their opponents are well prepared and
ready for combat. When it does come to battle, moreover, especially
during the summer, they make their attack at the hottest hour of the
day. They hope that the heat of the sun and the delay in beginning the
action will dampen the courage and spirit of their adversaries. They
then join battle with calmness and determination, marching step by
step in even and dense formation.

They are really bothered by cold weather, rain, and the south
wind, all of which loosen their bow strings. They are also disturbed
by a very carefully drawn-up formation of infantry, by an even field
with no obstacles to the charge of lancers, by hand-to-hand combat
and fighting because volleys of arrows are ineffective at close quarters, and because they themselves do not make use of lances and
shields. Charging against them is effective because they are prompted
to rapid flight and do not know how to wheel about suddenly against
their attackers, as do the Scythian nations. They are vulnerable to
attacks and encirclements from an outflanking position against the

flanks and rear of their formation because they do not station sufficient flank guards in their battle line to withstand a major flank attack. Often, too, unexpected attacks at night against their camp are
effective because they pitch their tents indiscriminately and without
order inside their fortifications.

To do battle against them our forces should be drawn up as prescribed in the book on formations. Select open, smooth, and level
terrain, if you can do so, without any swamps, ditches, or brush
which could break up the formation. When the army is prepared
and lined up for battle, do not delay the attack if you have really
decided to fight a pitched battle on that day. Once you get within
bowshot make the attack or charge in even, dense, regular order, and
do it quickly, for any delay in closing with the enemy means that
their steady rate of fire will enable them to discharge more missiles
against our soldiers and horses.

If it is necessary to fight a battle on very rough ground, it is better
not to have the whole battle line on horseback in such places, but to
draw some up in infantry formation while others remain mounted.
When lancers attack archers, as we have said, unless they maintain
an even, unbroken front, they sustain serious damage from the arrows and fail to come to close quarters. Because of this they require
more even ground for such fighting. If the army is not really ready
for combat, it must not engage in a pitched battle. Instead, employ it
safely in skirmishes and raids against the enemy, which can be done
smoothly on favorable terrain. Neither the enemy nor our own
troops should be allowed to discover the reason for putting off a
pitched battle, since it would embolden the one and make cowards
out of the other. Wheeling or turning around in withdrawals should
not be directed against the enemy's front, but to turn up their flanks
and take their rear. For the Persians pressing on in pursuits, make an
effort not to break up their formation, for this would easily expose
their rear to forces wheeling around against them. By the same
token, if a force withdrawing before them wants to turn about and
attack the front lines of the pursuing Persians, it will suffer injury on
running into their well-ordered ranks. For the Persians do not attack
in a disorderly fashion as the Scythians do in pursuing, but cautiously
and in good order. For this reason, as has been said, forces wheeling
about should not attack their front, but should be sure to go by the
flanks against their rear.

2. Dealing with the Scythians, That Is, Avars, Turks, and Others Whose Way of Life Resembles That of the Hunnish Peoples

The Scythian nations are one, so to speak, in their mode of life and in their organization, which is primitive and includes many peoples.[2] Of these peoples only the Turks and the Avars concern themselves with military organization, and this makes them stronger than the other Scythian nations when it comes to pitched battles. The nation of the Turks is very numerous and independent.[3] They are not versatile or skilled in most human endeavors, nor have they trained themselves for anything else except to conduct themselves bravely against their enemies. The Avars, for their part, are scoundrels, devious, and very experienced in military matters.

These nations have a monarchical form of government, and their rulers subject them to cruel punishments for their mistakes. Governed not by love but by fear, they steadfastly bear labors and hardships. They endure heat and cold, and the want of many necessities, since they are nomadic peoples. They are very superstitious, treacherous, foul, faithless, possessed by an insatiate desire for riches. They scorn their oath, do not observe agreements, and are not satisfied by gifts. Even before they accept the gift, they are making plans for treachery and betrayal of their agreements. They are clever at estimating suitable opportunities to do this and taking prompt advantage of them. They prefer to prevail over their enemies not so much by force as by deceit, surprise attacks, and cutting off supplies.

They are armed with mail, swords, bows, and lances. In combat most of them attack doubly armed; lances slung over their shoulders and holding bows in their hands, they make use of both as need requires. Not only do they wear armor themselves, but in addition the horses of their illustrious men are covered in front with iron or felt. They give special attention to training in archery on horseback.

A vast herd of male and female horses follows them, both to provide nourishment and to give the impression of a huge army. They

2. "Scythian" is a general term employed by Byzantine writers to designate the nomadic tribes north of the Black Sea and through the central Asiatic steppes. On the Avars, see B. Zástérová, *Les Avares et les Slaves dans la Tactique de Maurice* (Prague, 1971).
3. These would be the western Turks in the area east of the Black Sea and north of Persia: Wiita, "Ethnika," 122.

do not encamp within entrenchments, as do the Persians and the Romans, but until the day of battle, spread about according to tribes and clans, they continuously graze their horses both summer and winter. They then take the horses they think necessary, hobbling them next to their tents, and guard them until it is time to form their battle line, which they begin to do under cover of night. They station their sentries at some distance, keeping them in contact with one another, so that it is not easy to catch them by a surprise attack.

In combat they do not, as do the Romans and Persians, form their battle line in three parts, but in several units of irregular size, all joined closely together to give the appearance of one long battle line. Separate from their main formation, they have an additional force which they can send out to ambush a careless adversary or hold in reserve to aid a hard-pressed section. They keep their spare horses close behind their main line, and their baggage train to the right or left of the line about a mile or two away under a moderately sized guard. Frequently they tie the extra horses together to the rear of their battle line as a form of protection. They make the depth of their files indefinite depending on the circumstances, being inclined to make them deeper, and they make their front even and dense.

They prefer battles fought at long range, ambushes, encircling their adversaries, simulated retreats and sudden returns, and wedge-shaped formations, that is, in scattered groups. When they make their enemies take to flight, they put everything else aside, and are not content, as the Persians, the Romans, and other peoples, with pursuing them a reasonable distance and plundering their goods, but they do not let up at all until they have achieved the complete destruction of their enemies, and they employ every means to this end. If some of the enemy they are pursuing take refuge in a fortress, they make continual and thorough efforts to discover any shortage of necessities for horses or men. They then wear their enemies down by such shortages and get them to accept terms favorable to themselves. Their first demands are fairly light, and when the enemy has agreed to these they impose stricter terms.

They are hurt by a shortage of fodder which can result from the huge number of horses they bring with them. Also in the event of battle, when opposed by an infantry force in close formation, they stay on their horses and do not dismount, for they do not last long fighting on foot. They have been brought up on horseback, and owing to their lack of exercise they simply cannot walk about on their own feet. Level, unobstructed ground should be chosen, and a cavalry force should advance against them in a dense, unbroken mass to engage them in hand-to-hand fighting. Night attacks are also effective, with part of our force maintaining its formation while the other lies in ambush. They are seriously hurt by defections and desertions. They are very fickle, avaricious and, composed of so many tribes as they are, they have no sense of kinship or unity with one another. If a few begin to desert and are well received, many more will follow.

When they are moving up for battle, the first thing to do is have your scouts on the alert, stationed at regular intervals. Then make your plans and actual preparations in case the battle should not turn out well. Look for a good defensive position for use in an emergency, collect whatever provisions are available, enough for a few days for the horses as well as for the men, especially have plenty of water. Then make arrangements for the baggage train as explained in the book treating of that subject. If an infantry force is present, it should be stationed in the front line in the customary manner of the nation to which it belongs. The force should be drawn up according to the method shown in the diagram of the convex line of battle, that is, with the cavalry posted behind the infantry. If only the cavalry is ready for combat, draw them up according to the manner set down in the book on formations. Post a numerous and capable force on the flanks. In the rear the defenders are sufficient. When pursuing, the assault troops should not get more than three or four bowshots away from the formation of defenders, nor should they become carried away in the charge. When possible seek a clear and unobstructed area to form the battle line, where no woods, marshes, or hollows might serve as a screen for enemy ambushes. Post scouts at some distance from all four sides of the formation. If at all possible, it is helpful to have an unfordable river, marshes, or a lake behind the battle line, so that the rear is securely defended. If the battle turns out well, do not be hasty in pursuing the enemy or behave carelessly. For this nation does not, as do the others, give up the struggle when worsted in the first battle. But until their strength gives out, they try all sorts of ways to assail their enemies. If the formation is mixed, with most of it being infantry, it is still necessary to make provision for forage for the horses. When the enemy is approaching, by no means should the cavalry be allowed to send out foraging parties.

3. Dealing with the Light-Haired Peoples, Such As the Franks, Lombards, and Others Like Them

The light-haired races place great value on freedom. They are bold and undaunted in battle. Daring and impetuous as they are, they consider any timidity and even a short retreat as a disgrace. They calmly despise death as they fight violently in hand-to-hand combat either on horseback or on foot. If they are hard pressed in cavalry actions, they dismount at a single prearranged sign and line up on foot. Although only a few against many horsemen, they do not shrink from the fight. They are armed with shields, lances, and short swords slung from their shoulders. They prefer fighting on foot and rapid charges.

Whether on foot or on horseback, they draw up for battle, not in any fixed measure and formation, or in regiments or divisions, but according to tribes, their kinship with one another, and common interest. Often, as a result, when things are not going well and their friends have been killed, they will risk their lives fighting to avenge them. In combat they make the front of their battle line even and dense. Either on horseback or on foot they are impetuous and un-disciplined in charging, as if they were the only people in the world who are not cowards. They are disobedient to their leaders. They are not interested in anything that is at all complicated and pay little attention to external security and their own advantage. They despise good order, especially on horseback. They are easily corrupted by money, greedy as they are.

They are hurt by suffering and fatigue. Although they possess bold and daring spirits, their bodies are pampered and soft, and they are not able to bear pain calmly. In addition, they are hurt by heat, cold, rain, lack of provisions, especially of wine, and postponement of battle. When it comes to a cavalry battle, they are hindered by uneven and wooded terrain. They are easily ambushed along the flanks and to the rear of their battle line, for they do not concern themselves at all with scouts and the other security measures. Their ranks are easily broken by a simulated flight and a sudden turning back against them. Attacks at night by archers often inflict damage, since they are very disorganized in setting up camp.

Above all, therefore, in warring against them one must avoid engaging in pitched battles, especially in the early stages. Instead, make use of well-planned ambushes, sneak attacks, and stratagems. Delay things and ruin their opportunities. Pretend to come to agreements with them. Aim at reducing their boldness and zeal by shortage of provisions or the discomforts of heat or cold. This can be done when our army has pitched camp on rugged and difficult ground. On such terrain this enemy cannot attack successfully because they are using lances. But if a favorable opportunity for a regular battle occurs, line up the army as set forth in the book on formations.

4. Dealing with the Slavs, the Antes, and the Like

The nations of the Slavs and the Antes live in the same way and have the same customs.[4] They are both independent, absolutely refusing to be enslaved or governed, least of all in their own land. They are populous and hardy, bearing readily heat, cold, rain, nakedness, and scarcity of provisions.

They are kind and hospitable to travelers in their country and conduct them safely from one place to another, wherever they wish. If the stranger should suffer some harm because of his host's negligence, the one who first commended him will wage war against that host, regarding vengeance for the stranger as a religious duty. They do not keep those who are in captivity among them in perpetual slavery, as do other nations. But they set a definite period of time for them and then give them the choice either, if they so desire, to return to their own homes with a small recompense or to remain there as free men and friends.

They possess an abundance of all sorts of livestock and produce, which they store in heaps, especially common millet and Italian millet.[5] Their women are more sensitive than any others in the world. When, for example, their husband dies, many look upon it as their own death and freely smother themselves, not wanting to continue their lives as widows.

They live among nearly impenetrable forests, rivers, lakes, and marshes, and have made the exits from their settlements branch out

4. The author is undoubtedly writing of the Slavs bordering the Byzantine Empire along the lower Danube. The Antes lived to their northeast. What the *Strategikon* records about both peoples is confirmed by other sources: Wiita, "Ethnika," 259ff. See also Zástérová, *Les Avares et les Slaves.*
5. It seems clear that the first Greek word, *kenchros*, means common millet (*panicum miliaceum*), but some scholars would translate the second word, *elymos*, as barley or buckwheat. Wiita believes that a less robust grain called Italian millet (*setaria italica*) is meant: "Ethnika," 279–81.

in many directions because of the dangers they might face. They bury their most valuable possessions in secret places, keeping nothing unnecessary in sight. They live like bandits and love to carry out attacks against their enemies in densely wooded, narrow, and steep places. They make effective use of ambushes, sudden attacks, and raids, devising many different methods by night and by day. Their experience in crossing rivers surpasses that of all other men, and they are extremely good at spending a lot of time in the water. Often enough when they are in their own country and are caught by surprise and in a tight spot, they dive to the bottom of a body of water. There they take long, hollow reeds they have prepared for such a situation and hold them in their mouths, the reeds extending to the surface of the water. Lying on their backs on the bottom they breathe through them and hold out for many hours without anyone suspecting where they are. An inexperienced person who notices the reeds from above would simply think they were growing there in the water. But a person who has had some experience with this trick, recognizing the reeds by the way they are cut or their position, either shoves them down further into their mouths or pulls them out, which brings the men to the surface, since they cannot remain under water any longer without them.

They are armed with short javelins, two to each man. Some also have nice-looking but unwieldy shields. In addition, they use wooden bows with short arrows smeared with a poisonous drug which is very effective. If the wounded man has not drunk an antidote beforehand to check the poison or made use of other remedies which experienced doctors might know about, he should immediately cut around the wound to keep the poison from spreading to the rest of the body.

Owing to their lack of government and their ill feeling toward one another, they are not acquainted with an order of battle. They are also not prepared to fight a battle standing in close order, or to present themselves on open and level ground. If they do get up enough courage when the time comes to attack, they shout all together and move forward a short distance. If their opponents begin to give way at the noise, they attack violently; if not, they themselves turn around, not being anxious to experience the strength of the enemy at close range. They then run for the woods, where they have a great advantage because of their skill in fighting in such cramped quarters. Often too when they are carrying booty they will abandon

121

it in a feigned panic and run for the woods. When their assailants disperse after the plunder, they calmly come back and cause them injury. They are ready to do this sort of thing to bait their adversaries eagerly and in a variety of ways.

They are completely faithless and have no regard for treaties, which they agree to more out of fear than by gifts. When a difference of opinion prevails among them, either they come to no agreement at all or when some of them do come to an agreement, the others quickly go against what was decided. They are always at odds with each other, and nobody is willing to yield to another.

In combat they are hurt by volleys of arrows, sudden attacks launched against them from different directions, hand-to-hand fighting with infantry, especially light-armed troops, and having to fight on open and unobstructed ground. Our army, therefore, should comprise both cavalry and infantry, especially light-armed troops or javelin throwers, and should carry a large amount of missiles, not only arrows, but also other throwing weapons. Bring materials for building bridges, the kind called floating, if possible. In this way you may cross without effort the numerous and unfordable rivers in their country. Build them in Scythian manner, some men erecting the framework, others laying down the planks. You should also have ox-hide or goatskin bags to make rafts, and for use in helping the soldiers swim across for surprise attacks against the enemy in the summer.

Still, it is preferable to launch our attacks against them in the winter when they cannot easily hide among the bare trees, when the tracks of fugitives can be discerned in the snow, when their household is miserable from exposure, and when it is easy to cross over the rivers on the ice. Most of the animals and superfluous equipment should be left behind in a very safe place with a suitable guard and officer in charge. The dromons should be anchored at strategic locations. A moira of cavalry under outstanding officers should be stationed in the area as a protection so that the army on the march shall not be distracted in the event of hostile ambushes, and also to spread rumors that an attack against the enemy is being planned in some other location. By means of such a rumor and the anxiety of their chiefs, each of whom will be worried about his own problems, they will not have the opportunity to get together and cause trouble for our army. Do not station these troops close to the Danube, for the enemy would find out how few they are and consider them unimportant. Nor should they be very far away, so their will be no delay, if it becomes necessary, to have them join the invading army. They should stay about a day's march from the Danube. This army should cross over into enemy territory suddenly and make its invasion on clear and level ground. Immediately a competent officer should ride ahead with some picked men to take captives from whom it will be possible to get information about the enemy. As far as possible, avoid marching through rough or wooded terrain during summer until thorough reconnaissance has been made, and, in case the enemy is present in force, until they have been driven away by our infantry or cavalry. If we have to march through a narrow pass, and if we expect to return by the same route, measures must be taken, as explained in the book dealing with this matter, to clear the way, widen the road, or to leave a relatively strong force behind in the area to prevent the enemy from hiding and making surprise attacks which could over-whelm our army on its return when it is likely to be encumbered with plunder.

As much as possible, avoid making camp in thickly wooded areas or pitching your tents near such places. For they can easily serve as a base for launching attacks or for rustling horses. The infantry force should encamp in order and within the fortification. The cavalry should encamp outside, with sentinels posted in a wide circle around the grazing horses, unless it is possible to bring in forage for the horses, so they can stay inside day and night.

If an opportunity for battle occurs, do not make your battle line against them too deep. Do not concentrate only on frontal attacks, but on the other sectors as well. Suppose that the enemy occupy a fairly strong position and have their rear well covered so that they do not allow us an opportunity to encircle them or to attack their flanks or their rear. In that event it is necessary to post some troops in concealment, have others simulate a flight before their front, so that, lured by the hope of pursuit, they may abandon their good defensive position, and then our men will turn back against them, while those in hiding come out and attack them.

Since there are many kings among them always at odds with one another, it is not difficult to win over some of them by persuasion or by gifts, especially those in areas closer to the border, and then to attack the others, so that their common hostility will not make them united or bring them together under one ruler. The so-called refu-

123

gees who are ordered to point out the roads and furnish certain information must be very closely watched.[6] Even some Romans have given in to the times, forget their own people, and prefer to gain the good will of the enemy. Those who remain loyal ought to be rewarded, and the evildoers punished. Provisions found in the surrounding countryside should not simply be wasted, but use pack animals and boats to transport them to our own country. The rivers there flow into the Danube, which makes transportation by boat easy.

Infantry are necessary not only in narrow passes and fortified places, but also in rough country and along rivers. Even in the face of the enemy it is then possible to bridge over them. When a small force of infantry, both heavy and light, has been secretly brought across at night or during the day and immediately drawn up in formation, keeping their backs to the river, they provide enough security to put a bridge across the river. In cramped river crossings or in defiles it is necessary for the rear guard to be ready for action at all times, disposed according to the terrain. For one may expect attacks to occur whenever the force is divided, and the troops who are advancing cannot aid those in the rear. Surprise attacks against the enemy should be carried out according to standard procedure. One detachment approaches their front and provokes them, while another detachment, infantry or cavalry, is posted secretly in the rear on the route by which they are expected to flee. The enemy then who avoided action or who flee from the first attacking force will unexpectedly run right into the other detachment. In summer there must be no letup in hurting them. During that time of year we can pillage the more open and bare areas and aim at entrenching ourselves in their land. This will aid the Romans who are captives among them to gain their freedom, after escaping from them. The thick foliage of summer makes it fairly easy for prisoners to escape without fear.

The procedures of the march, the invasion, and the pillaging of the country, and other more or less related matters, are dealt with in the book on invading hostile territory. Here the subject will be summarized as best as possible. The settlements of the Slavs and Antes lie in a row along the rivers very close to one another. In fact, there is

6. During the reign of Heraclius refugees from the Danube regions, Pannonia, Dacia, and Dardania sought safety in Thessalonica: *Les plus anciens recueils des miracles de Saint Démétrius et la pénétration des slaves dans les Balkans*, ed. P. Lemerle (Paris 1979), 1: 20–21, 185.

practically no space between them, and they are bordered by forests, swamps, beds of reeds. As a result, what generally happens to invasions launched against them is that the whole army comes to a halt at their first settlement and is kept busy there, while the rest of the neighboring settlements, on learning of the invasion, easily escape with their belongings to the nearby forests. Their fighting men then come back ready for action, seize their opportunities, and attack our soldiers from cover. This prevents the invading troops from inflicting any damage on the enemy. For these reasons we must make surprise attacks against them, particularly in unexpected places. The bandons or tagmas must be so arranged beforehand that they know which one is first, which second, which third, and they should march in that order through very constricted areas, so they do not get mixed up and lose time in reorganizing themselves. When a crossing has been made without detection, if there are two suitable places which can be attacked, the army ought to be divided in two, with the lieutenant general taking one part, ready for battle and without a baggage train, and advance a distance of fifteen to twenty miles through unsettled land on their flanks with a view to launching an attack from the more mountainous areas. Then on approaching the settlements there, he should begin the pillaging, continuing until he meets the units with the general. The general, keeping the other part of the army, should invade and pillage from the other end of the settlements. Both should be advancing, destroying, and pillaging the settlements between them until they meet up with one another in a determined place. On arriving there they should pitch camp together toward evening. In this way the attack is successfully carried out. The enemy running away from one detachment will unexpectedly fall right into the hands of the other, and they will not be able to regroup.

If there is only one suitable road by which it is possible to invade the settlements, the army should still be divided. The lieutenant general must take half or even more of it, a strong force and ready for battle, without a baggage train. His own bandon, with himself in his proper place, should advance at the head of the whole force, and accompanying him should be all the tagma commanders. When his force approaches the first settlement, he should detach one or two bandons so, while some go about pillaging, others may keep guard over them. It is wise not to detach too many bandons for the first settlements, even if they happen to be large ones. For when our army arrives, there is no time for the inhabitants to organize any resis-

125

tance. The lieutenant general should continue his advance rapidly, while still carrying out the same procedure at the rest of the settlements along the way as long as there are enough tagmas under his command. The lieutenant general himself ought to stay clear of all these actions. He should retain for himself three or four bandons, up to a thousand capable men, until the invasion is completely finished, so he can see to reconnaissance and security for the rest of the troops.

While the lieutenant general is discharging these duties, the general should follow along, have the pillaging troops join him, and keep moving up toward the lieutenant general. For his part, the lieutenant general should turn back and gather up the pillagers along his line of march. In the place where the two encounter each other they should set up camp together that same day. These surprise incursions made by the two units should not advance more than fifteen or twenty miles, so that both may get there, do their pillaging, and pitch camp on the same day. In these expeditions those of the enemy able to put up resistance need not be taken alive, but kill everyone you encounter and move on. When you are marching along do not let them delay you, but take advantage of the opportunity.

Now then, we have reflected on these topics to the best of our ability, drawing on our own experience and on the authorities of the past, and we have written down these reflections for the benefit of whoever may read them. All the other topics which one is likely to encounter and which are not written about in the present book must be examined in the light of what we have written, of the teachings of experience, and of the very nature of things, and, as far as possible, applied to problems as they arise. For how would it be possible for us or for anyone else to write about everything that might come up in the future? How write about what the enemy will try next or will always do? Who can tell how many things the future will bring? They do not all campaign according to the same school of thought. Generalship is a very diversified art; many different methods of combat are employed. This means that one must devote some time imploring God for the ability to use his talents to outwit the enemy. Human nature is very cunning and beyond comprehension; it is able to conceive many plans and to act in devious ways.

· B O O K X I I ·
[Mixed Formations, Infantry, Camps, and Hunting]

A. MIXED ORDER OF BATTLE

1. Formation of a Mixed Order of Battle. List of Symbols for the Units in a Mixed Force

♂	The General of the whole army
Φ	The Lieutenant General
᷉	Merarch of the cavalry
Ṅ	Merarch of the infantry
᷄	Moirarch of the cavalry
✝	Bandon of assault troops
♂	Bandon of defenders
τ	Heavy-armed infantryman
ι	Light-armed infantryman, archer, javelin thrower
Κ	Cavalryman

2. The Order of Battle Called Mixed

infantry meros	cavalry meros	infantry meros	cavalry meros	infantry meros	cavalry meros	infantry meros
τ τ Ñ τ τ	✝ ⅄ ♂ⅿ ♂⅄ ✝	τ τ Ñ τ τ	✝ ⅄ ♂ ♂ ♂⅄✝	τ τ Ñ τ τ	✝ ⅄ ♂ⅿ ₒ ⅄ ✝	τ τ Ñ τ τ
τ τ τ τ τ	K K K K K K K	τ τ τ τ τ	K K K K K K K	τ τ τ τ τ	K K K K K K K	τ τ τ τ τ
τ τ τ τ τ	K K K K K K K	τ τ τ τ τ	K K K K K K K	τ τ τ τ τ	K K K K K K K	τ τ τ τ τ
τ τ τ τ τ	K K K K K K K	τ τ τ τ τ	K K K K K K K	τ τ τ τ τ	K K K K K K K	τ τ τ τ τ
τ τ τ τ τ	K K K K K K K	τ τ τ τ τ	K K K K K K K	τ τ τ τ τ	K K K K K K K	τ τ τ τ τ
τ τ τ τ τ	K K K K K K K	τ τ τ τ τ	K K K K K K K	τ τ τ τ τ	K K K K K K K	τ τ τ τ τ
τ τ τ τ τ	K K K K K K K	τ τ τ τ τ	K K K K K K K	τ τ τ τ τ	K K K K K K K	τ τ τ τ τ

phalanx   phalanx

τ τ τ τ τ   τ τ τ τ τ

τ τ τ τ τ   τ τ τ τ τ

τ τ τ τ τ   τ τ τ τ τ

τ τ τ τ τ   τ τ τ τ τ

τ τ τ τ τ   τ τ τ τ τ

ι ι ι ι ι   ι ι ι ι ι

This formation is suitable for fighting against cavalry when the cavalry force is of the same size, or even smaller, than the infantry force.

128

3. The First Order of Battle for Cavalry

```
K K K K K K K K K K
K K K K K K K K K K
K K K K K K K K K K
K K K K K K K K K K
K K K K K K K K K K
K K K K K K K K K K
K K K K K K K K K K
K K K K K K K K K K


K K K K K K K K K K
K K K K K K K K K K
K K K K K K K K K K
K K K K K K K K K K
K K K K K K K K K K
K K K K K K K K K K
K K K K K K K K K K
K K K K K K K K K K
```

This formation is suitable for fighting against cavalry when our cavalry outnumber our infantry, but is of the same strength as that of the enemy. In this case form two lines of cavalry and one of infantry. Make certain that the lines are about an arrowshot apart from one another. The cavalry should form its lines in both extended and close order.

SECOND ORDER OF BATTLE OF INFANTRY

```
τ τ τ τ τ τ τ τ τ τ τ τ
τ τ τ τ τ τ τ τ τ τ τ τ
τ τ τ τ τ τ τ τ τ τ τ τ
τ τ τ τ τ τ τ τ τ τ τ τ
τ τ τ τ τ τ τ τ τ τ τ τ
τ τ τ τ τ τ τ τ τ τ τ τ
τ τ τ τ τ τ τ τ τ τ τ τ
τ τ τ τ τ τ τ τ τ τ τ τ
ι ι ι ι ι ι ι ι ι ι ι ι
```

4. Another Formation

```
K K K K K K K        т т т т т т т т т т        K K K K K K K
K K K K K K K        т т т т т т т т т т        K K K K K K K
K K K K K K K        т т т т т т т т т т        K K K K K K K
K K K K K K K        т т т т т т т т т т        K K K K K K K
K K K K K K K        т т т т т т т т т т        K K K K K K K
K K K K K K K        т т т т т т т т т т        K K K K K K K
K K K K K K K        т т т т т т т т т т        K K K K K K K
K K K K K K K        т т т т т т т т т т        K K K K K K K
```

cavalry rearguard   *cavalry rearguard*

```
т т т т т т т т                               т т т т т т т т
т т т т т т т т                               т т т т т т т т
т т т т т т т т                               т т т т т т т т
т т т т т т т т                               т т т т т т т т
т т т т т т т т                               т т т т т т т т
т т т т т т т т                               т т т т т т т т
т т т т т т т т                               т т т т т т т т
т т т т т т т т                               т т т т т т т т
ɾ ɾ ɾ ɾ ɾ ɾ ɾ ɾ                               ɾ ɾ ɾ ɾ ɾ ɾ ɾ ɾ
ɾ ɾ ɾ ɾ ɾ ɾ ɾ ɾ                               ɾ ɾ ɾ ɾ ɾ ɾ ɾ ɾ
```

This formation is suitable for fighting against infantry when our own infantry outnumber the cavalry.

130

5. The Order of Battle Called Lateral

τ τ τ τ τ τ   τ τ τ τ τ τ   τ τ τ τ τ τ   τ τ τ τ τ τ

τ τ τ τ τ τ   τ τ τ τ τ τ   τ τ τ τ τ τ   τ τ τ τ τ τ

τ τ τ τ τ τ   τ τ τ τ τ τ   τ τ τ τ τ τ   τ τ τ τ τ τ

τ τ τ τ τ τ   τ τ τ τ τ τ   τ τ τ τ τ τ   τ τ τ τ τ τ

τ τ τ τ τ τ   τ τ τ τ τ τ   τ τ τ τ τ τ   τ τ τ τ τ τ

τ τ τ τ τ τ   τ τ τ τ τ τ   τ τ τ τ τ τ   τ τ τ τ τ τ

τ τ τ τ τ τ   τ τ τ τ τ τ   τ τ τ τ τ τ   τ τ τ τ τ τ

τ τ τ τ τ τ   τ τ τ τ τ τ   τ τ τ τ τ τ   τ τ τ τ τ τ

ι ι ι ι ι ι   ι ι ι ι ι ι   ι ι ι ι ι ι   ι ι ι ι ι ι

ι ι ι ι ι ι   ι ι ι ι ι ι   ι ι ι ι ι ι   ι ι ι ι ι ι

This is suitable in bare and unobstructed places.

6. Formation in a Column

τ τ τ

τ τ τ

τ τ τ

τ τ τ

τ τ τ

τ τ τ

τ τ τ

τ τ τ

front τ τ τ

τ τ τ

τ τ τ

τ τ τ

τ τ τ

τ τ τ

τ τ τ

τ τ τ

τ τ τ

τ τ τ

This is necessary for passing through defiles, rough terrain, and thickly wooded country. It can be formed in lines of two, three, and four, all in column according to the lay of the land.

7. The Formation Called Convex

How should the mixed or convex formation be drawn up? For what is it useful?

The depth of the phalanx and the order of battle must be formed in accord with the strength and the nature of the force. If there is more cavalry than infantry, the cavalry files can be made as deep as eight or even ten men, whereas the infantry should be more shallow, four or five men. If there is more infantry than cavalry, form them in exactly the reverse order. A convenient proportion for such formations is one-third cavalry and two-thirds infantry. Even if the cavalry makes up only a fourth, the army will not be unbalanced. If we are warring against a foreign and powerful nation and our army is in good shape, it is wise, I believe, in the first fighting, in that period when we are getting used to the enemy, to form the foot soldiers in files of eight heavily armed men and two lightly armed, and to make the cavalry formation eight or ten deep, and this should withstand any enemy attempt to charge or break our ranks. But when our troops get roused up to take the offensive against the enemy, then a depth of four heavily armed foot soldiers and one lightly armed is enough, for with the cavalry right behind them, this formation cannot easily be broken. The flank guards should be about a thousand or a thousand two hundred on both sides, and the rear guard in square formation should be about five hundred, heavy- and light-armed men. In disposing troops the so-called wedge formation of infantry can be useful for the rear guard. Orders should be given to the cavalry that if the infantry push back their adversaries and turn them to flight, then at a signal the files of foot soldiers which had been ahead of the cavalry go into their deep formation with their company commanders or primi and leave a gap in their line. Then the cavalry comes out through the gap at a steady pace and in good order so as not to trample the infantry. As soon as they have passed by the files of the phalanx, the leading half of each cavalry file should take up a faster but still uniform gait, as best they can, and ride after the retreating enemy for three or, at the most, five bowshots, but no farther because of enemy ambushes. The second half of each cavalry file should follow along in order, forming a close, even front. Then, in case the horsemen who have ridden on ahead should be turned back, this second group, still in formation, will be able to receive them. The infantry phalanx should also follow along in formation. It is not a bad idea to attach a cavalry tagma or so to the infantry flank guards on both sides, so they can support them in case of need. Also, if all the cavalry in the force move out in pursuit of the enemy, they too may gallop out and get close to the cavalry flanks, but to the rear, forming themselves into flank guards for it. The infantry, as noted, is already covering the rear. In the event that neither the horsemen who first rode up ahead nor those in the second group are able to check an enemy countercharge and retreat through the rear of the line of infantry, then these flank guards come and station themselves abreast of the line of infantry, but not along the front to avoid disorder and confusion. Then the infantry comes out of the deep formation of the files it had gone into, and the force again fills the gaps in the line and stands to resist the enemy. If the enemy advances to within bowshot and attempts to charge and break up our phalanx, a very dangerous move for them, the infantry should close ranks in the regular way. The first, second, and third men in each file form a foulkon,[1] interlocking their shields, fix their spears firmly in the ground, holding them inclined forward and straight outside their shields, so that anyone who dares come too close will quickly experience them. They also lean their shoulders and put their weight against the shields to resist any pressure from the enemy. The third man, who is standing nearly upright, and the fourth man hold their spears like javelins, so when the foe gets close they can use them either for thrusting or for throwing and then draw their swords. The light-armed infantry and the cavalry use the bow. If the enemy should try to move against the cavalry from the rear, something they generally attempt, the infantry divides into a double phalanx. Every second file drops out to the rear, passing between the cavalry units, and the cavalry stays there in the middle. The light-armed infantry are also divided, half of them go with the forward phalanx, and half with the phalanx to the rear. The squares also provide support for the rear.

To prevent the formation from being too closely observed by the enemy before the battle, a thin screen of cavalry may be deployed in front of the infantry phalanx until the enemy gets close. When they are about four or five bowshots from the battle line, this cavalry screen leaves the infantry files to rejoin the rest of the cavalry at its place back in the line, and this group forms as the front rank of the

1. *Foulkon*, related to German *Volk*, is a very close formation like the old Roman *testudo*: see H. Mihăescu, "Les termes de commandement militaires latins dans le Strategicon de Maurice," *Revue de linguistique* 14 (1969): 261–72.

cavalry, as shown in the attached diagram. The results are that the line is securely protected, and that the enemy will approach very boldly, thinking they have to do with cavalry only, and they will be easily beaten as the infantry all of a sudden charge out in the way we have explained. This sort of formation requires constant practice for both men and horses to get accustomed to doing it. It must be understood just how far afield the cavalry can go in their pursuits riding fast and without confusion, and not letting the infantry formation become unduly disordered or thinned out. This formation is basic when infantry accompany a cavalry force, with or without wagons, or for cavalry by themselves. Should the cavalry find themselves in a critical situation because of difficult terrain or a reverse in battle and become very nervous, then some of them can pick up the shields of the heavy infantry, if they have lost their own, and line up in formation on foot, while others remain mounted in the manner explained above, and in this way the danger may be averted.

*LIST OF SYMBOLS USED FOR THE TROOPS DRAWN UP
IN A MIXED OR CONVEX FORMATION*

T   Front-rank infantryman, file leader, dekarch

O   Heavy-armed infantryman with shield, man-at-arms

I   Light-armed infantryman, javelin thrower, archer

K   Cavalryman

DIAGRAM OF A MIXED FORMATION, THE CONVEX ONE, CONTAINING BOTH HORSE AND FOOT, WHICH IS ESSENTIAL IN CRITICAL SITUATIONS

phalanx

```
  T T T T T T T T      T T T T T T T T T T T T T T T T T T      T T T T T T T T
 ⊢0 0 0 0 0 0 0 0      0 0 0 0 0 0 0 0 0 0 0 0 0 0 0 0 0 0      0 0 0 0 0 0 0 0⊣
 ⊢0 0 0 0 0 0 0 0      0 0 0 0 0 0 0 0 0 0 0 0 0 0 0 0 0 0      0 0 0 0 0 0 0 0⊣
 ⊢0 0 0 0 0 0 0 0      0 0 0 0 0 0 0 0 0 0 0 0 0 0 0 0 0 0      0 0 0 0 0 0 0 0⊣
 ⊢0 0 0 0 0 0 0 0      0 0 0 0 0 0 0 0 0 0 0 0 0 0 0 0 0 0      0 0 0 0 0 0 0 0⊣
 ⊢0 0 0 0 0 0 0 0      0 0 0 0 0 0 0 0 0 0 0 0 0 0 0 0 0 0      0 0 0 0 0 0 0 0⊣
 ⊢0 0 0 0 0 0 0 0      0 0 0 0 0 0 0 0 0 0 0 0 0 0 0 0 0 0      0 0 0 0 0 0 0 0⊣
 ⊢0 0 0 0 0 0 0 0      0 0 0 0 0 0 0 0 0 0 0 0 0 0 0 0 0 0      0 0 0 0 0 0 0 0⊣
 ⊢0 0 0 0 0 0 0 ⊢⊢     I I I I I I I I I I I I I I I I I I     ⊢⊢0 0 0 0 0 0 0⊣
 ⊢0 0 0 0 0 0 0 ⊢⊢     I I I I I I I I I I I I I I I I I I     ⊢⊢0 0 0 0 0 0 0⊣
 ⊢0 0 0 0 0 0 0 ⊢⊢                                            ⊢⊢0 0 0 0 0 0 0⊣
 ⊢0 0 0 0 0 0 0 ⊢⊢                                            ⊢⊢0 0 0 0 0 0 0⊣
 ⊢0 0 0 0 0 0 0 ⊢⊢                                            ⊢⊢0 0 0 0 0 0 0⊣
 ⊢0 0 0 0 0 0 0 ⊢⊢                                            ⊢⊢0 0 0 0 0 0 0⊣
 ⊢0 0 0 0 0 0 0 ⊢⊢                                            ⊢⊢0 0 0 0 0 0 0⊣
 ⊢0 0 0 0 0 0 0 ⊢⊢                                            ⊢⊢0 0 0 0 0 0 0⊣
 ⊢0 0 0 0 0 0 0 ⊢⊢                                            ⊢⊢0 0 0 0 0 0 0⊣
 ⊢0 0 0 0 0 0 0 ⊢⊢                                            ⊢⊢0 0 0 0 0 0 0⊣
 ⊢0 0 0 0 0 0 0 ⊢⊢                                            ⊢⊢0 0 0 0 0 0 0⊣
 ⊢0 0 0 0 0 0 0 ⊢⊢                                            ⊢⊢0 0 0 0 0 0 0⊣
 ⊢0 0 0 0 0 0 0 ⊢⊢                                            ⊢⊢0 0 0 0 0 0 0⊣
 ⊢0 0 0 0 0 0 0 ⊢⊢                                            ⊢⊢0 0 0 0 0 0 0⊣
 ⊢0 0 0 0 0 0 0 ⊢⊢                                            ⊢⊢0 0 0 0 0 0 0⊣
  K K K K K K K K K                                            K K K K K K K K K
  K K K K K K K K K                                            K K K K K K K K K
  K K K K K K K K K                                            K K K K K K K K K
  K K K K K K K K K                                            K K K K K K K K K
  K K K K K K K K K                                            K K K K K K K K K
```

flank guards (left) · *flank guards* (right)

square, infantry rearguard   square, infantry rearguard

```
  T T T T T                          T T T T T
  0 0 0 0 0                          0 0 0 0 0
 ⊢0 0 0 0 0⊣                        ⊢0 0 0 0 0⊣
 ⊢0 0   0 0⊣                        ⊢0 0   0 0⊣
 ⊢0 0 0 0 0⊣                        ⊢0 0 0 0 0⊣
  0 0 0 0 0                          0 0 0 0 0
  ↓ ↓ ↓ ↓ ↓                          ↓ ↓ ↓ ↓ ↓
```

B. INFANTRY FORMATIONS

Next we have to discuss infantry tactics, a subject which has been long neglected and almost forgotten in the course of time, but one which we think deserves the greatest attention. We are concerned with treating of their training and also of their armament and dress, and everything else regarding the traditional formation and organization of such troops. We have collected material on these subjects and now transmit them in writing to the officers concerned, so they may know them and put them into practice. To make it more convenient for them, we have now arranged the subject matter in the form of an index, and throughout we have been much more concerned with practicality and brevity than with style. We have compiled a list of the chapter headings and have drawn up the following outline of our treatise.

CONTENTS OF THE TREATISE ON INFANTRY FORMATIONS

1. Clothing to Be Worn by the Infantry

The infantry soldiers should wear either Gothic tunics coming down to their knees or short ones split up the sides. They should have Gothic shoes with thick soles, broad toes, plain stitching, and fastened with no more than two clasps; the soles should be studded with a few small nails for greater durability. Boots or greaves are not required, for they are unsuitable for marching and, if worn, slow one down. Their mantles should be simple, not like the Bulgarian cloaks. Their hair should be cut short, and it is better if it is not allowed to grow long.

2. Training of the Individual Heavy-Armed Infantryman

They should be trained in single combat against each other, armed with shield and staff, also in throwing the short javelin and the lead-pointed dart a long distance.

3. Training of the Light-Armed Infantryman or Archer

They should be trained in rapid shooting with a bow, using a lance set up a good distance away as a target. They can shoot in either the Roman or the Persian manner. They should be trained in shooting rapidly while carrying a shield, in throwing the small javelin a long distance, in using the sling, and in jumping and running.

138

4. Armament. Weapons of the Heavy-Armed Infantryman

The men of each arithmos or tagma should have shields of the same color, Herulian swords, lances, helmets with small plumes and tassels on top and on the cheek plates—at least the first men in the file should have these—slings, and lead-pointed darts. The picked men of the files should have mail coats, all of them if it can be done, but in any case the first two in the file. They should also have iron or wooden greaves, at least the first and last soldier in each file.

5. Weapons of the Light-Armed Infantryman

They should carry bows on their shoulders with large quivers holding about thirty or forty arrows. They should have small shields, as well as crossbows with short arrows in small quivers.[2] These can be fired a great distance with the bows and cause harm to the enemy. For men who might not have bows or are not experienced archers, small javelins or Slavic spears should be provided. They should also carry lead-pointed darts in leather cases and slings.

6. Essential Equipment to Be Kept in Mind and Gotten Ready Beforehand

There should be light wagons, one to each dekarchy or squad, no more, or men will be too busy with them and neglect other matters. Each wagon should carry a hand mill, an ax, hatchets, an adz, a saw, two picks, a hammer, two shovels, a basket, some coarse cloth, a scythe, lead-pointed darts, caltrops tied together with light cords attached to an iron peg so they can be easily collected. There should be other wagons carrying revolving ballistae at both ends, also the artillery crews, carpenters, metal workers, all under a single officer. Packhorses should be apportioned, if possible, one to each squad, or at least one to every two squads. If the opportunity arises for the foot soldiers to leave the wagons and seize some position, these beasts should be used to carry rations for eight or ten days, and they can accompany the troops until the slower wagons arrive. Still other wagons are needed to carry the weapons and arms of each arithmos.

2. J. Haldon, "Solenarion—The Byzantine Crossbow," *Historical Journal of the University of Birmingham* 12 (1970): 155–57; G. Dennis, "Flies, Mice, and the Byzantine Crossbow," *Byzantine and Modern Greek Studies* 7 (1981): 1–5.

Ten or even twenty others should carry flour or biscuits, arrows, and spare bows.

7. The Soldiers from Each Arithmos Who Are to Be Assigned to Specialized Duties

Heralds should be alert, intelligent, with vigorous, pleasant voices, able to speak Latin, Persian if possible, and Greek. There should be drill masters, standard bearers or draconarii, trumpeters, armorers, weapon makers, bowmakers, arrow makers, and the rest according to regulations.[3] Certain men should be assigned the duty of collecting lost articles and returning them to their owners. Just as in the cavalry baggage train, certain men should be placed in charge of the wagons, whom the men in the baggage train should obey, and in each meros one in command of all the trains. Just as with the horses, a special mark should identify the oxen which belong to each arithmos so the men can easily recognize them. It is also very important, if possible, to have two eagle bearers.[4]

8. Organization of the Infantry Army and Its Officers

In the past, when the legions were composed of large numbers of men, the authorities formed the heavy infantry company or tagma from sixteen files, 256 men. Each file, then, consisted of sixteen men, and the whole battle line comprised sixty-four companies or 1,024 files for a force of sixteen, 384 men, in addition to 8,000 light-armed troops such as archers, javelin throwers, and slingers, and 10,000 cavalrymen. They divided both the heavy and the light infantry com-

3. Drill master: *campiductor* or *campidoctor*: Vegetius, *Ep. rei. milit.*, 1, 13; 2, 23. Draconarius is the bearer of the dragon symbol, which seems to have disappeared from the Roman armies by the sixth century. It is not clear whether the draconarius here is anachronistic or still had some function; R. Grosse, "Die Fahnen in der römisch-byzantinischen Armee des 4.–10. Jahrhunderts," *Byzantinische Zeitschrift* 24 (1924): 359–72.
4. Eagle bearer, *ornithoboras*, literally "bird bearer," with bird perhaps evolving as did the American military slang of bird colonel from the eagle insignia of rank. This probably derives from the old Roman *aquilifer*, the soldier who bore the eagle-topped standard of the legion. Plutarch renders it as *aetophoros*. Other spellings (e.g. *orniboras*) and interpretations do not make much sense. The Ambrosian paraphrase calls the soldier an *ordinator*. His duties were probably those of an aide-de-camp or orderly, and he was supposed to be unarmed.

panies into four equal contingents, right, left, left center, right center, and the cavalry into two groups. But since our present units are not even equal in strength, it is not easy to fix a definite number for a company. It could end up with men in excess of 256 having nothing to do or, if made to serve with soldiers whom they did not know, they might become disoriented. It seems better to make the numerical strength of the unit flexible. Depending on the manpower available, make one large unit or two smaller ones. Each tagma should have its own standard and commanding officer. Ordinarily he should be a tribune, respected, intelligent, and good at hand-to-hand fighting, but he may also be a lieutenant or drill master. At any rate, make sure that the files of each tagma are always sixteen deep, organized according to their duties. Make the battle line in proportion to the strength of the whole army. Divide this line, all the tagmas and files present, into four equal contingents, right under the command of the right merarch or stratelates, left under the command of the left merarch or stratelates, left center under the command of the left center merarch or stratelates, right center under the command of the right center merarch or stratelates. A few soldiers, both heavy and light infantry with their own officers, not really needed in the battle line, should be held in reserve to provide quick assistance in emergencies either on the flanks of the line beyond the cavalry, or by the wagons, or in other places. If the army consists of less than 24,000 foot soldiers, divide it into three, not four, contingents. In the center meros raise the general's standard, which all the others should use as a guide.

9. Assignments of Personnel and Organization of the Infantry Tagma

First, those who know how to shoot with the bow or who are able to learn, and who are young and strong, should be selected for the light-armed infantry. If there are more than 24,000 men in the army, half should be selected, if less, a third in each company. They should be organized into dekarchies with competent dekarchs over them, and an officer known as the chief archer. The other half of the company should be divided into files of eighteen men, both veterans and recruits. The two poorest may be assigned to duty with the wagons or elsewhere as needed. The sixteen left should be placed in the battle line under the command of respected and intelligent file leaders.

Of the sixteen, the eight most competent are stationed in the front and in the rear of the file, that is, positions one, two, three, four, and sixteen, fifteen, fourteen, thirteen. In this way even if the depth of the file is reduced to four, its front and rear will still be strong. The remaining men, the weaker ones, should be stationed in the center of the file.

Of these sixteen, every other man should be listed as primi or secundi. Two should bear a double listing, that is, the first should be called file leader and primus, the other dekarch and secundus. From these the rest will then be designated as primi and secundi. To make it easier to command them and get them to operate more harmoniously as a unit, it is necessary to divide them into two squads. The primi go with the file leader, the secundi with the dekarch. In this manner, even though they may be temporarily divided, nonetheless in formation these sixteen soldiers are unified and subject to the decisions and will of the file leader. As a result, good order and discipline are easily maintained.

All of the heavy- and light-armed troops should be divided and drawn up in four equal contingents. If practicable, it is helpful to arrange the sixteen men in each heavy infantry file not only according to their qualifications, but also according to stature. By stationing the taller men in front, the whole line will look much better ordered and impressive. But if they cannot be ranked according to stature and manliness, then the better soldiers in each file should, as we have said, be stationed to the front and to the rear, with the weaker ones in the middle in the manner described.

For good reasons, then, our predecessors fixed the depths of the files for combat at sixteen. It provides an adequate number of troops, which should not be exceeded, and when necessary it can be divided quickly and in an orderly fashion and reduced to only one man.

10. Instructions to Be Given About Punishments

After the army has been organized as described above, it should be assembled in its entirety one day. If the soldiers and officers already know the regulations set down by law, simply remind them. Otherwise they should be read to the troops separately in each tagma by their own commanders, as we explained in the chapters dealing with the cavalry.

11. Formation of the Heavy Infantry Tagma

After the regulations have been promulgated, the organization of each tagma should be completed by its officers. First, the files of the tagma are assigned their positions, some drawn up to the left, some to the right of the standard or of the commander. The commander himself then moves forward together with the standard bearer, the herald, the drill master, and the trumpeter. The file leaders follow in their assigned positions, first those on the left side, then those on the right. On arriving at the site of the battle line, the commander halts with the standard bearer right behind him and behind them the orderly and the trumpeter. The files draw up on both sides of them in their assigned positions far enough apart so they will not bump into one another, keeping the depth at sixteen, with the light-armed troops to the rear. They hold the points of their spears high to avoid any inconvenience. The drill master and the herald march in front of the line, the one for reconnaissance and guide duty, the other to transmit orders from the commander. If a tagma is being drilled, its commanding officer should take up his position in front with the herald and drill master. If a meros is being drilled, nobody should be out in front except the commander of the meros, mounted, with two heralds, two drill masters, one strator, one spatharios, and two eagle bearers.[5] They stay there until the battle line gets close to the point of fighting. Then all return to the ranks to the place where their standard is unfurled. The commander should not personally engage the enemy in combat, nor should the eagle bearers, who are unarmed. No trumpet or bugle, no matter how many there are, should sound in each meros except that of the merarch, otherwise the resulting confusion may prevent the orders from being heard.

12. Formation of the Light Infantry with Heavy Infantry and Cavalry

The light infantry is formed in several different ways. Sometimes the archers are posted to the rear of each file in proportion to the number of men, that is, four for the sixteen heavy foot soldiers, so that if the heavy infantry ranks are reduced to four deep in a file, there will

5. Strator, spatharios: apparently aides.

be one archer behind it. Sometimes they are placed within the files, alternating one heavy-armed infantryman with one archer. Sometimes they are placed among the files and on the flanks of the line, that is, on the inside of the cavalry. Frequently, if there is a large number of them, they are placed a short distance to the outside of the cavalry, along with a few heavy-armed infantry as a flank guard for the cavalry stationed there. The troops with the small javelins or darts should be either behind the heavy infantry files or on the flanks of the line, not in the middle. At present we form the archers and others with missiles behind the files for drill.

13. Formation of Cavalry with Heavy Infantry

The cavalry should be formed on the flanks of the infantry line, the best tagmas under their own officers farther out. If the cavalry force is large, that is, over 12,000, they should be about ten deep; if less than that, about five. An extra detachment should be posted for their support to the rear, outside the wagons. In case some of the enemy approach from that direction, they can repel them or, if no such need arises, they may support the flanks of the line. Their formation should be a very open one, so they do not run into one another when the time comes for wheeling about.

The cavalry should be ordered not to race after the enemy or to get too far away from the infantry line, even if the enemy turns in flight. They might run into an ambush and, by themselves, few in numbers, far from any assistance, they may be badly beaten. If they should be driven back by the enemy, they should take refuge in the rear of the battle line, but not go beyond the wagons. If they still cannot hold out, they should dismount and defend themselves on foot.

If the army wants to draw up for battle, but not actually engage in fighting that day, and the enemy charges against our cavalry, who may not be able to resist, they should not await the charge in their position on the flanks of the line, but should move in behind the infantry, that is, between the line and the wagons. To facilitate such a movement, the distance between the line and the wagons should be greater, so the cavalry may not be cramped in any maneuvers they may have to make and may not be injured by the enemy's arrows.

144

14. Infantry Drill Movements

The herald commands: "Silence. Observe orders. Do not worry. Keep your position. Follow the standard. Do not leave the standard and pursue the enemy."[6] The troops then advance at a steady pace and in silence, without anyone even whispering. They should become accustomed to these movements, so that at a spoken command, a nod, or some other signal, they march or halt, reduce or divide the depth of the files, march steadily in close order for a good distance over various kinds of terrain, close or tighten their ranks in depth and width, march in a foulkon,[7] engage in a mock battle, sometimes using staffs and sometimes naked swords.

15. A Second Drill

They should divide into a double phalanx and then resume normal formation, face to the right and the left, march to the flank and then back to their original position, change their front to the right and to the left, broaden and thin their formation, deepen or double the depth of the files, change their front to the rear and then back again.

16. How to Begin the Above Movements

These maneuvers are begun as follows. The troops march or halt at a spoken command, a nod, or some other signal. When he wants them to march, the drill master signals by trumpet, horn, or voice, and they march. To halt, the signal is given by trumpet, voice, or movement of the hand, and they halt. It is essential that the troops become accustomed to these commands by voice or signal, so they will not be confused by the clash of arms, dust, or fog.

The files, which are ordinarily sixteen men deep, may be thinned or divided, for example, when the commander wants to extend the width of the battle line, either to make it look more impressive or to have it the same width as that of the enemy. He gives the command: "By eights," or: "March out."[8] They then divide with every other

---

6. Silentium. mandata captate. non vos turbatis. ordinem servate. bando sequute. nemo demittat bandum et inimicos seque.
7. See Book XII, n. 1.
8. Ad octo. exi.

man stepping out of line, and the depth of the files is reduced. The width of the battle line is extended, and the depth becomes eight men. If he wants to make it four deep, he again orders: "March out."[9] As above, they all step to one side, either right or left. Make sure that all step in or out to one side.

They should march evenly in close order. So, when some men in the line step out in front and the whole line becomes uneven, the command is given: "Straighten out the front."[10] And the front is made even.

They tighten up or close ranks when the line gets to about two or three bowshots from the enemy's line and they are getting set to charge. The command is: "Close ranks."[11] Joining together, they close in toward the center, both to each side and to front and back, until the shields of the men in the front rank are touching each other and those lined up behind them are almost glued to one another. This maneuver may be executed either while the army is marching or while it is standing still. The file closers should order those in the rear to close in forcefully on those to the front and to keep the line straight, if necessary, to prevent some from hesitating and even holding back.

They move in a foulkon when the two lines, ours and the enemy's, are getting close, and the archers are about to open fire, and the front-rank men are not wearing coats of mail or knee guards. The command is: "Form foulkon."[12] The men in the front ranks close in until their shields are touching, completely covering their midsections almost to their ankles. The men standing behind them hold their shields above their heads, interlocking them with those of the men in front of them, covering their breasts and faces, and in this way move to attack.

When ranks have been properly closed, and the line is about one bowshot from the enemy, and the fighting is just about to begin, the command is given: "Ready."[13] Right after this another officer shouts: "Help us." In unison everyone responds loudly and clearly: "O God."[14] The light-armed troops start shooting their arrows over-

9. *Exi.*
10. *Dirige frontem.*
11. *Junge.*
12. *Ad fulcon.*
13. *Parati.*
14. *Adiuta . . . Deus.* Silver coins of Heraclius for the year 615 bear the inscrip-

146

head. The heavy infantry, who are drawn up in the front line, advance still closer to the enemy. If the men have darts or missile weapons, they throw them, resting their lances on the ground. If without such weapons, they advance more closely, then hurl their lances like javelins, take out their swords and fight, each man remaining in his proper position and not pursuing the enemy if they turn to retreat. The men to the rear keep their heads covered with their shields and with their lances support those in the front. Obviously, it is essential for the soldiers in the first line to keep themselves protected until they come to blows with the enemy. Otherwise, they might be hit by enemy arrows, especially if they do not have coats of mail or greaves.

They are divided into a double phalanx when the line is advancing straight ahead and hostile forces appear both in front and to their rear. Assuming that the files are sixteen men deep, if the enemy approaching the front is getting very close and about to begin fighting, give the command: "Divide in the middle. Form double phalanx." [15] The first eight men halt. The other eight face about and move back, thus forming a double phalanx. If the files are eight deep or even four, then the command is: "Primi halt, secundi march out. Form double phalanx." [16] The secundi, those under the dekarch, face about and march out a distance of three hundred paces or feet, far enough so the enemy's arrows will not cause harm to the rear of either phalanx but will fall in the clear space between them. "Return." [17] They again turn around, if the need arises, and return to their previous formation. If, as may occur, the larger hostile force approaches the rear of our line and the wagons are not following behind, then the secundi halt and the primi march out. The double-phalanx formation is appropriate when the wagons are not following or have been seized by the enemy.

Facing to the right or the left is called for when the commander wants to move the line by the flank to one side either, as would be likely, to extend the line and outflank the enemy, to avoid being outflanked by them, to obtain more favorable ground, or to pass a defile. If he wants to march it to the right, he orders: "To the lance,

---

tion: *Deus adiuta Romanis*: H. Goodacre, *A Handbook of the Coinage of the Byzantine Empire* (London, 1957), 95–99.

15. *Medii partitis ad difallangiam.*
16. *Primi state, secundi ad difallangiam exite.*
17. *Reverte.*

face." [18] Each soldier, then, remaining in place, turns. "March." [19] And they move to the designated place. "Return." [20] And they resume their original front. If he wants them to go to the left, he orders: "To the shield, face. March." [21] And the rest is observed as above. The two-faced line is called for in the event that the enemy suddenly circles around both front and rear before our battle line has time to divide into the double phalanx. Give the command: "Face in all directions." [22] Half of the troops stand fast to meet the enemy attacking from the front. The other half turns about to the rear. The middle ranks remain in place with their heads covered by their shields.

They change front to the right or the left when the commander wants to bring our battle line to the right or left to meet some emergency which might arise. The command for this is: "Change to the right, or the left." [23] By one tagma at a time changing front, the whole line is quickly brought over to the designated front.

The line can be made more open or broadened. When the soldiers are in close order and the commander wants, as he might on occasion, to divide or thin out the files and extend the width of the battle line or give it more slack, he gives the command: "Move out to both sides." [24] And they broaden out. This maneuver can be executed while the line is marching or has come to a halt, with both flanks heading to the outside, and can be done by a single meros or the whole line.

The depth of the files may be increased or doubled. Assume that the troops are standing four deep and the commander wants to double that to correspond to the depth of the enemy's line and to make his own stronger in preparation for the charge. The command for this is: "Enter." [25] And the files become eight deep. If he wants to make them sixteen deep, he gives the same command: "Enter." One by one they return to their own position, and the files are doubled, resuming their original depth as one unit of sixteen men. Although this is generally not advisable, still, in case the

18. *Ad conto clina.*
19. *Move.*
20. *Redi.*
21. *Ad scuto clina, move.*
22. *Undique servate.*
23. *Depone au dextra au senestra.*
24. *Largia ad ambas partes.*
25. *Intra.*

commander wants to make the files thirty-two deep, he orders: "File in file."[26] They are doubled in the manner described above, and the battle line is deepened while its width is reduced.

When the line is marching on straight ahead, and the enemy, instead of coming to them from the front, approach from the rear, the line may be turned around. If the commander wants to bring the front, that is, the file leaders, around to the rear, the files still being sixteen deep, he orders: "Change place."[27] The line stands still while the file leaders pass through the files to the rear; the rest of the men follow behind them, and they form a new front facing the enemy. It is best to do this before they close ranks. But if they are already closed, and there is no time to open them, the command is given: "About face."[28] Remaining in position, each man turns around to the rear, and the sixteenth man, the file closer, is now in front instead of the file leader.

17. Formation of the Battle Line and Practice in Resisting the Enemy

After drilling of each individual tagma has been satisfactorily completed in the manner described above, the whole army should be brought together and drawn up in full array as though for a pitched battle. There should be heavy and light infantry, cavalry, wagons, and the rest of the baggage train. Lined up on the other side and forming a simple line opposed to them should be either infantry or cavalry firing arrows without points. This simple line should sometimes move in formation against our battle line, sometimes raising dust, shouting, and in disorder, sometimes from behind, or attacking our flanks or rear. In this way, our soldiers, foot and horse, will become accustomed to all kinds of conditions and not be disturbed by them, and the merarchs will gain facility in meeting attacks. The cavalry should receive similar training, sometimes stationed on the flanks, sometimes moving to the rear of the infantry, and then facing about.

The divisions are drawn up in the battle line with intervals of one or two hundred feet between them, so they will not be crowded together while marching, but can still act in unison during

26. *Acia in acia.*
27. *Muta locum.*
28. *Transforma.*

battle and provide support for each other. They should be instructed to use the center meros as a guide, for it is there that the standard of the general is posted. It was for this reason that military men in the past referred to the center of the battle line as the mouth or the navel, because the rest of the formation followed its lead.

Since it is quicker and safer to close or tighten ranks than to open or broaden them, the initial formation of the files need not be sixteen deep, but only four. This makes our battle line look more impressive to the enemy, and it also makes our soldiers more relaxed while marching, especially if it is for some distance. If the need should arise to make the line eight or sixteen deep, this type of closing can be done quickly on the march. On the other hand, if the formation is already tight and close and the need arises to extend its width, many hours are required for this. It is not wise, moreover, to extend the line when the enemy is close.

The standard bearers, mounted, should remain with their commanders until the battle line has been formed, then they take their position in the formation on foot. No matter how deep or how shallow the enemy's files are, the depth of our own files should not exceed sixteen men, nor should it be less than four. More than sixteen is useless, and less than four is weak. The middle ranks consist of eight heavily armed infantry. Absolute silence must be observed in the army. The file closers of each file should be instructed that if they hear so much as a whisper from one of their men, they should prod him with the butt of their lance. In combat, also, they should push forward the men in front of them, so that none of the soldiers will become hesitant and hold back. The foot soldiers should not be expected to march long distances in full armor. In case their adversaries delay matters, and the battle line has to wait around, they should not be forced to stand for many hours. If they do, by the time the fighting begins, they will be already worn out because of the weight of their armament. They should, instead, be made to sit down and rest. Only when the enemy gets close should they be called to attention, and they will be fresh and in good condition. Nobody should march out in front of the battle line except the merarchs, mounted, each accompanied by two heralds, two drill masters, one strator, one spatharios, and two eagle bearers. They should stay there until the enemy gets close, then each should take position in his own meros.

Bear in mind that it is very good and practical to have the infantry force or its individual units become accustomed to the signs or commands used in their drills, for it makes the soldiers more obedient and ready for action. In battle it is not necessary for the whole line to maneuver at one signal. For the terrain or the situation does not always permit this, especially since the line is composed of so many men and extends such a distance. The signals which have to be given in certain situations would not be clear to all the troops. Besides, the movements of the enemy are not uniform. Suppose, for example, that one unit in the line is shallow and is being pushed back by the enemy. Other units, whose ranks are deeper, may be able to assist. If one unit is surrounded by the enemy, the others may form on a double front and help it out. For these reasons each unit must adapt the movements described earlier to the formations of the force which is attacking it and not wait for some other signal. In fact, for all to halt or to march uniformly in obedience to a single command is necessary only up to the moment of contact. Because of this our predecessors divided large armies into various units and tagmas.

18. Arrangement of the Wagons and the Baggage Train

If it was decided to have the wagon train follow along, it should be stationed a full bowshot behind the infantry force with each section accompanying its own meros in good order. The wagons should occupy the same extent of ground as is covered by the battle line, for if they extend beyond it, they cannot be protected. Each wagon should have its back part covered by heavy cloth, so that the drivers can stand up and fight as though from behind a rampart, and the oxen will be protected from the hail of arrows. The ballista-carrying wagons should be distributed along the whole front, with most, including the most powerful, stationed on the flanks. The drivers should be able to use javelins, slings, metal darts, or arrows. The rest of the baggage train should be in between the wagons. The area between the line of troops and the wagons should be kept clear, so that in case the heavy infantry has to divide into the double phalanx because of an attack upon the wagons, either the cavalry or the light-armed troops can race through without the wagons presenting an obstacle or causing confusion. If a strong, hostile force harasses the wagons from behind, and the drivers are not able to hold them off, and neither are the troops in the double phalanx, then throw out a few

151

caltrops. In that case, though, be careful that the army does not return by the same route, but by another, so it will not be injured by them.

19. Method of Marching with the Enemy Nearby

Cavalry patrols should be sent out in front and to the rear, and none of the infantry should be allowed beyond the line of patrols. The camp sites should be fairly close, so that the infantry does not become worn out from marching long distances. The wagons should be arranged according to each meros of the army, either in column or in line, depending on the nature of the ground. First should be the wagons of the right meros, then those of the left, then of the left center, and finally of the right center. There should be no confusion or mixing of different sections. If the enemy is nearby, the soldiers should not leave their weapons in the wagons, but should carry them as they march along, so they may be ready to fight. In times of pressure, they should march in the order of their battle formation, tagma by tagma, without any mixing of units or spreading out. If it then becomes necessary to form the battle line, they are already in a good position to do so. If the enemy cavalry force is large and is getting close to our army, we should not change camp sites or undertake a march until after the battle is over. Instead, two or three days beforehand we should occupy the place where the battle is likely to take place and there set up camp with due precautions.

20. Traversing of Wooded Areas, Rough Terrain, and Narrow Passes by Infantry

For a successful expedition against an enemy in wooded areas, rough terrain, and narrow passes, especially against the Slavs and Antes, the troops should be lightly equipped and without many horsemen. They should march without wagons; their baggage train should not be large nor should they have heavy armament such as helmets and mail coats. The heavy-armed troops should carry moderate-sized shields, short spears, not the kind used by the cavalry; the light-armed men should have smaller shields, lighter bows and arrows, short spears, short Moorish javelins, and some metal darts. They should get all the available axes and have them carried by the pack animals for use when needed. The heavy infantry force should not be drawn up in a straight line or front as in flat and open country, but, depending on the size of the force, into two or four units, two or four ranks deep. It should march by the flank, as shown in the diagram below, adapting to the needs of the situation, and its units should march along staying about a stone's throw apart. If cavalry or baggage trains are present, the trains should be placed in the rear, followed by the cavalry, and behind them should be a few heavy and light infantry as a rear guard to ward off likely surprise attacks from the rear. Some of the light infantry, accompanied by a small unit of cavalry, should proceed about a mile ahead of the main body. Others should march on both flanks to patrol and to discover any enemy ambushes. They should look carefully for trees which seem to be standing upright, but which have been sawed partway through, so they can be quickly pushed over to block those narrow places in which a surprise attack can cause serious trouble. The light infantry, accompanied by a few horsemen, should be on the alert for such stratagems and, at the same time, should clear out any enemy troops in hiding. The main body may then pass through.

Where the country is fairly open, the cavalry should ride in advance to patrol, but where it is thick and difficult, the light infantry. The light infantry ought not be drawn up in close order as is the heavy infantry, but in irregular groups, that is, three or four armed with javelins and shields so they may protect themselves if necessary while hurling the javelin. They should also have one archer to provide covering fire for them. These little groups, as remarked above, should not march along in one solid formation, nor should they be widely scattered, but they should be one after the other to protect each other's rear. If something should happen to the leading group, if, for example, they encounter resistance from the enemy or get bogged down in rough terrain, the groups behind them may move up to higher ground without being observed and come down upon the enemy's rear. This must always be the objective of the light-armed troops, to seize higher ground and get above the enemy. The light infantry should be instructed not to go any further from the main body than where they can hear its trumpets or bugles. Otherwise they may well find themselves cut off from support and be overpowered. Suppose that the four divisions of the main body, who are marching along by the flank, come to a spot so narrow that all four cannot pass. Then two divisions should fall back and form a double column. If the place is too narrow for two divisions, then have one at a time pass, lining itself up in one column by the flank, and the rest following, always, of course, keeping the light-armed troops out in front. After passing the narrow place, they resume their original formation of four units or divisions marching by the flank.

If a strong enemy force appears in front of them or off to the side, they must form the front of the battle line in that section which is threatened. If, for example, the enemy appears to the left of the column, the meros on that flank halts in position, and the other three come and line up in their proper positions relative to it. If the enemy appears to the right, the corresponding maneuver is made and the front formed in that direction. If they appear in front of either one or both of the center divisions, the other two head toward the right, deploying from a column into a line, and form for battle with their flank as the front. If the terrain permits our troops to march in close order against the enemy, then the light-armed infantry and cavalry should circle around the enemy. But if the close-order formation is not practicable, then line up the heavy infantry files more in depth and with wider gaps between them, so they can easily make their way through wooded areas and, if need be, resume close order. If even this is not feasible, the main body should halt while the light infantry, closely supported by a few heavy-armed men and cavalry, should be sent out against the enemy.

Instructions should be given to the army that in the event that while it is marching along an alarm is sounded that the enemy is nearby, the whole army should not become excited and race toward that section. The heavy-armed troops should maintain their formation, while the light infantry dashes toward the man who gave the alarm. The troops in front should not hastily move to the flanks, nor those on the flank to the front except as ordered by their commanding officer. Each meros should support its own troops in times of alarm, as each situation demands. In the event that the troops are being hard pressed, they should hurry back to the main body of heavy infantry, so they will not be overwhelmed by the enemy. Infantry, therefore, is able to undertake a march in safety and good order, as we have said, in thickly wooded and difficult country if they march by the flank, either in four divisions or two, depending on the terrain, and in more open country using a formation with the front on the flank if they keep their files fairly wide and deep.

It should be borne in mind that in thickly wooded country, javelin throwers are needed more than archers or slingers. For this reason, most of the light infantry should be trained in using javelins and short spears. Archers, rather, are needed in close connection with the main battle line and in rough, steep, narrow, and open country. Javelin throwers, for their part, should be stationed away from the main line and are particularly needed in thickly wooded areas.

The security of our entrenchments and camps is important. If possible, the tents should be pitched in open country, but if this cannot be done, we cannot become careless. Our camps should be tightly guarded and strong. Avoid those places which have higher ground close by. Do not dismiss the main body of troops until everyone has pitched his tent, and the camp is properly fortified, and patrols have been sent out. Everyone must remember that the blast of the bugle is the signal to halt and the blast of the trumpet the signal to march.

We have appended some sketches for a clearer understanding of the formations described in this chapter.

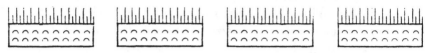

front

Lateral formation, which looks impressive and is useful in open country

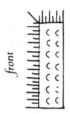

Formation in a single column or phalanx, which is basic and suited for use in narrow passes and where there is only one road.

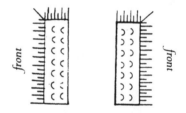

Formation in line using a double phalanx, which is essential for thickly wooded areas, and for providing refuge and a rallying point for the light infantry and cavalry, as well as protection for the baggage trains.

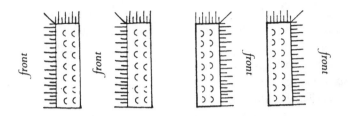

Formation in line using four phalanxes, which is basic when the infantry force is very large, and the ground is favorable and in case we want to traverse an area more quickly and it also makes it easier to change front to flank.

21. River Transportation. Crossing Rivers in the Face of the Enemy

Everything must be gotten ready beforehand, the fighting ships and the other ships and gear, supply ships, smaller boats, materials for making bridges, including the struts and pontoons. The fleet should be organized just as an army for marching on land. It should be commanded by moirarchs, merarchs, and the proper officers for the various tagmas comprising it. Each warship should bear a regular standard on its masthead to make it clear which officer is in command. Next, one admiral or general should be placed in command of the fleet. If there are a large number of warships, divide them into three divisions, each under a commanding officer, and each with a trumpeter and heralds. On the prows of all, or at least most, of the fighting ships, mount small ballistae, covered with heavy cloth, so their fire may repel any attacks by the enemy while they are still a good distance away. Good, competent archers should be assigned to the ships, and fortified positions constructed for them. When it is time to sail, all the new camp sites should be determined; the warships sail in order according to their divisions and keeping their prearranged formation and, as mentioned, when assembled at the designated place, and when it is clear that everyone is safe and accounted for, they then sail in formation to the next camp site. Since it is not always certain that they will be able to load the nets and heavier gear on the warships, the ships carrying these should be organized under their own officers as the baggage train is on land. Do not set up the camps too far apart, since the heavier ships might not get there in

time. They should encamp and set sail at the same time as the warships. The heavier ships should sail along behind the warships, and
behind them should be a few other ships to protect them. If it is
necessary to encamp on land when the enemy is nearby, be sure to
make a solid entrenchment to ward off any surprise attacks the enemy is likely to attempt at night. If a naval battle is imminent, and the
enemy appears lined up to fight, then draw up our fighting ships in a
single line abreast and have them sail ahead evenly just far enough
apart to avoid getting in one another's way, colliding, or banging their
oars together. This line should be long enough to occupy the whole
navigable width of the river safely. The ships, to repeat, should
be formed on a broad front, and any other ships present should be
posted in a second and a third line about a bowshot to the rear.

In the event that we should have to seize the opposite bank on
which the enemy is drawn up, then we would have to bridge it, that
is, construct a bridge. We have to begin on our bank by collecting
the materials required, including large skiffs, and then put down the
beams to construct a deck, presuming, of course, that everything,
beams and pontoons, has been gotten ready. As the bridge being
constructed gets to within a bowshot of the opposite bank, move out
the ballistae-carrying warships or all the vessels equipped with ballistae and use them to clear out the enemy. In this way, the building
of the bridge may be completed safely section by section until dry
land is reached. After it has been secured to the shores on both sides,
then, especially on the side where the enemy is, for further defense
of the bridge put up towers of wood, brick, or dry stone. First,
though, dig strong entrenchments to be occupied by infantry with
ballistae, so that the building of the towers can be completed without
hindrance. The army can then cross over, including cavalry or baggage trains.

22. Setting Up Fortified Camps

The wagons should be parked around the camp site, and in emergencies they should be dug in if the ground permits. Outside them a
ditch should be dug, five or six feet wide and seven or eight deep,
with the earth thrown up on the inner side. Outside the trench caltrops should be scattered and small pits dug with sharp stakes set in
the bottom. The location of all these should be made known to the
troops, since they might otherwise be injured. Along the circuit of
the camp there should be four large public gates and a number of

smaller ones. The commanding officer of the unit encamped closest to each gate or door should be responsible for guarding it. Just inside the line of wagons should be the small tents of the light-armed troops, and next to them a good, clear space of three or four hundred feet, and then the rest of the tents should be pitched. When the enemy starts shooting, then, their arrows will not reach the men in the middle, but will fall in the clear space. Two broad streets should run through the camp in the shape of a cross intersecting in the middle. They should be about forty or fifty feet wide, and on both sides should be the tents lined up in rows with a little space between them. Each merarch should camp in the middle of his troops. The general's tent should be off to one side, not at the central crossroads, so that it will not interfere with the flow of traffic, and that he himself will not be bothered by troops passing by. If the situation is such that the cavalry are to be inside the camp, they should be located in the middle and not near the edge.

The more competent tribunes with the tagmas under their command should be stationed at the gates of the camp, so that from the evening dismissal to reveille, nobody in camp may pass in or out without the general's permission. When the cavalry stays inside the camp, special attention should be given to the night patrols.

The commanding officer of each meros should keep one of his heralds in attendance at the general's tent, and each tribune should have a herald at the merarch's tent. This will expedite the transmission of orders for everyone.

Trumpeters and buglers should be on duty with the general. The trumpets should sound three times in the evening as a signal for work to cease; the men should then have supper and chant the "Thrice Holy." Some of the general's own troops should be detailed to inspect the guards and to enforce silence throughout the camp, so that nobody would even dare call out the name of his comrade. There are many advantages to keeping silence, for example, it often makes it possible to detect enemy spies lurking in the camp. Likewise, noise can lead to a great deal of trouble. Dancing and handclapping should be forbidden, especially after the evening dismissal, not only because they are disorderly and annoying, but they are a waste of energy for the soldiers. When the army is to move, orders should be given the evening before. Then, at dawn on the designated day the bugle should blow three times, and the march begins. The units move out in order, first the heavy-armored infantry, and then the wagons.

The use of caltrops is essential. If the ground is rocky and impossible to dig, or if it is late, caltrops properly scattered about accomplish the same purpose for the army in camp as do entrenchments.

Ancient authorities have described for us various shapes for a camp or entrenchment, but the present writer recommends the four-sided, oblong form as basic and making for good order. Camps situated on a broad front and on high ground make the army look more impressive than those on level or sloping ground. If, therefore, we want to impress enemy scouts, we should select sites with a broad front, especially if they have the supplies and provisions we need.

Healthy, clean places should be chosen for camps, and we should not stay too long in one spot, unless the air and the availability of supplies are more advantageous. Otherwise, disease can spread among the troops. It is very important that sanitary needs not be taken care of inside the camp, but outside because of the disagreeable odor, especially if there is some reason for the army to remain in one place.

In critical situations we should choose a site with a small river flowing through the middle of the camp for the convenience of the troops. But if it is large and swift, it is better left on the flank to help in protecting the army.

When the cavalry camp inside, special attention should be paid to the night patrols.

If a good-sized river flows by the camp, the horses must not be watered above the camp. If they are, their trampling around will make the water muddy and useless. They should be watered downstream instead. If it is a small stream, water the horses from buckets; if brought to the stream, they will only stir it up.

Camp should not be made near hills which are accessible to the enemy, for from them they can easily fire arrows into the encampment.

Before getting near the enemy, we should try not to make camp near water. This is particularly true for the cavalry. Horses and men can get in the habit of drinking a great deal of water, and when it is not available, they cannot stand it and lose heart.

Before getting near the enemy, the infantry should not camp mixed in with the cavalry inside the entrenchments. But the cavalry should stay outside, although close to the camp, so they may not be cramped for room and may not strike enemy spies as being few in number. It should be determined a few days beforehand, though, how much space they will require and how they are to be quartered if the situation should demand that they come inside the camp. When the enemy is near, they should join the infantry and should camp together with them in fixed sections. Around the time of combat, care should be taken to locate the camp in a strong position and to pay attention to supplies for a few days, not only provisions for the men but, if possible, also for the animals, for the outcome of battle is uncertain. Above all, give special thought to ways of defending the water supply against the enemy in case the camp is needed for support.

If the site of the battle is a wide, open place, always try to have a river, a lake, or some other natural obstacle to protect your rear. Make a strong camp and have the wagons follow the troops in order. If the ground is difficult and uneven, leave the trains and the rest of the baggage in the camp with a few wagon drivers as a guard, and form the battle line near the camp in a suitable place. If the ground is difficult, especially when the enemy is mounted, the difficult ground by itself is a good protection for our main body. If the wagons accompany the troops in that sort of country, not only will they be useless, but they will be very much in the way.

Care must be taken with the oxen pulling the wagons, so that while they are accompanying the army, and the wagons have to halt, they may not be frightened by the noise made by the enemy or by the arrows flying about and panic and throw the line into confusion. They should be hobbled or tied, so that, as mentioned, if some of them are wounded by arrows, they may not cause confusion among the infantry. For this reason they should not be stationed very close to them.

When the need arises to relieve a position under attack or to seize a place quickly, and the wagons would not arrive in time and would only slow things down, they should be left in a strong place, and the foot soldiers should go on ahead with their provisions; arrangements should be made to have them carried in packs on camels or on horses requisitioned for this purpose. They should also bring a supply of caltrops along with them. When the time comes to set up camp, they dig the entrenchments in the usual way, scatter the caltrops about, and to the inside build a wall or wooden palisade all around. This will provide as much protection as the wagon train did, and it will not slow them down or cause any of the other problems which it often does.

If there is a very large proportion of cavalry in the army and only a few infantry, and it is decided to have the baggage train remain in the camp, do not have all the infantry stay inside the camp. Some should be kept on guard duty there, while others should be posted in formation outside the gates and the entrenchments. Then, in case the cavalry should be driven back without having infantry with them, these infantry can cover them and give them the opportunity to turn back against the enemy or at least to enter the camp in good order and not be dangerously crowded together at the gates.

23. Matters to Be Considered by the Infantry General on the Day of Battle

If the enemy cavalry are very numerous, outnumbering our own, and our troops are not accompanied by their baggage train, do not plan on forming for battle in open and level country, but in rugged and difficult land, swampy places, rocky, uneven, or wooded.

Take care to send out patrols to keep our rear and flanks protected against attack.

Station a few extra heavy-armed infantry by the flanks and in the center of the wagons, so that, if necessary, they may help out in case the enemy plans on causing trouble around the wagons, or to the battle line, or to our cavalry.

Do not involve many cavalry in infantry battles, but just a few on the flanks of the battle line. There may be up to three or four thousand of them, but it is not safe to have more; they should be good soldiers and wearing coats of mail. If the opportunity presents itself, their duty is to attack retreating enemy units.

If the enemy army consists of cavalry and is reluctant to get into a battle with infantry, and if our own cavalry force is strong, whereas our infantry is weak, then line up three divisions of cavalry in front, and have the infantry battle line follow in good order about one or two miles behind them. Order the cavalry not to separate themselves from the infantry line any greater distance than that. If they are forced back by the enemy, they should retreat by way of the flanks and rear of the battle line and not by the front, which might cause it to break.

On the day of battle make sure not to march the infantry battle line a long distance, no more than two miles away from the camp, so they do not become worn out by the weight of their armor. If the enemy delays the battle, have the men sit down and rest until they are about to get close. If the weather is hot, let them take off their helmets and get some air. On such occasions they must not carry wine with them, for it will only make them warm and dull their minds. Water, however, should be carried in the wagons and given to each individual who needs it as they remain in formation.

24. Synopsis of the Above Drills Which Should Be Known by the Tribunes or Commanders of Infantry Tagmas

The herald shouts the following commands: "Attention to orders, so you will not disrupt the battle line. All eyes on the standard. Let none of you leave it. But pursue the enemy evenly and in order."[29] The troops march calmly, silently, at a steady pace, holding on high the points of their lances. They should become used to maneuvering at a signal, whether by voice or gesture, to march and to halt, to thin out or divide their ranks. The command is given: "Leave the file." They march steadily and in close order for a distance. If the front of the tagma is uneven, the command is: "Straighten the front." To reduce or tighten depth and width, the command is: "Close ranks." To march the command is: "Form foulkon." They should simulate single combat, sometimes with staffs, sometimes with naked swords. One man shouts: "Help us," and all respond in unison: "O God."

SECOND DRILL

To form the double phalanx, the command is given: "Primi stand in place, secundi step out." To move to the right and left. If the commander wants them to go to the right, he orders: "Right face." If to the left: "Turn and move to the left." And they move. "Return." And they resume their original position. For the double-faced defensive line the command is: "Face in all directions." Then they resume their original position. To change front to the right or the left. If to the right: "Change to the right." If to the left: "Change to the left." To extend or widen. If the commander wants the line extended to the right, he orders: "Extend to the right." If on both sides: "Extend on both sides." To increase or double the depth of the files. If they are eight or four deep, he commands: "Enter." To face to the rear. The command is: "About face."

29. The Laurentian manuscript gives these orders in Greek, while the others give them in Latin. The following orders simply repeat those given above.

Written regulations regarding these maneuvers should be given to the tribunes, and the merarchs should also know the purpose of the movements.

C. DIAGRAM OF A FORTIFIED CAMP

It should be noted that the line outside the wagon train indicates a trench. Caltrops are shown by the letter lambda, and the signs in the middle stand for the tents. The cross-shaped main streets should be fifty feet wide, the space around the wagons two hundred. A ditch should be dug outside the caltrops, so that animals or men in the camp may not unknowingly be entangled in them.

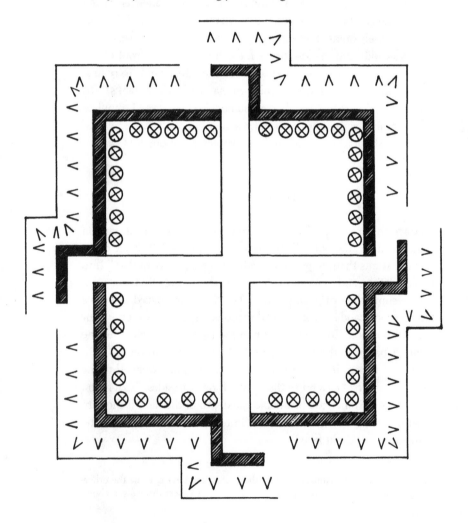

D. HUNTING. HUNTING WILD ANIMALS WITHOUT SERIOUS INJURY OR ACCIDENT

Devoting some time to hunting is of great value to the soldiers; not only does it make them more alert and provide exercise for their horses, but it also gives them good experience in military tactics. It is very important for them to become experts at it by constant practice during suitable and convenient times of the year, when the inexperienced can easily learn, and those who make mistakes, as one would expect, can be corrected without causing harm. Since divine providence has brought into being so many quick-witted and fleet-footed wild animals who run under their own leaders, it is only fitting that attacks on them should be made with some degree of tactics and strategy.

The formations should not be very deep, or they will be too short and occupy so small a space that they will be ineffective in rounding up game. Neither should they be too extended with the soldiers a good distance apart, or the game will slip through the gaps in the formation and be lost. In flat and open country the line may be extended as much as seven or eight miles, but no more; in fairly level but thick country the distance should be less.

It is important to set a limit to the number of horsemen who can fit in each mile in formation but organized loosely enough so they do not bump into each other and get mixed up while riding about. Allow up to eight hundred or a thousand horsemen to each mile.

The day before the hunt a few scouts should go looking for the game and should study the ground carefully. The commanders of each unit should then give orders to their troops. Once the line has been formed, everyone must move quietly and in order. Nobody should leave his assigned place, even if he encounters difficult ground. Nobody should spur his horse on or shoot when he is not supposed to. If, however, some game is chased out, the first man to come within bowshot should shoot at it, without leaving his place in the ranks. One of the heralds should then turn the dead game over to the tagma commander, and nobody else should dare touch it. If, because of some carelessness, the game gets away, that person who is responsible for letting it escape ought to be punished.

Nobody should ride out in front of the line except the merarchs with their own heralds and the tagma commanders with their heralds. The merarchs should distribute their heralds along the whole front of each meros to transmit the orders of the general and the reports from the scouts as they come in. The tagma commanders should maintain the alignment of their own tagmas.

On the day of the hunt, then, before the second hour, the army moves out to the hunt. The men should be equipped with light weapons such as bows and, for those who are not experienced in archery, spears. Some of the scouts go on ahead to observe the game, while others guide the army. When the game is close, about three or four miles away, begin to form in line in a suitable, protected location. Do not do it any closer for fear that because of the blowing of the wind and the movement of the army, the animals, whose senses are sharp, will very quickly catch the scent of the soldiers and will run away. The army should be drawn up in phalanx formation in three sections, center, right, and left, with flank guards stationed a little behind, but close to the flanks of the line. The depth of the files, as we have noted, will depend on the strength of the army, the nature of the ground, and the distance to be covered. They could be four, two, or even one horseman deep. The scouts arrive and lead the flanks of the line, whose duty it is to circle around the game to surround it completely. The line begins to move in the normal phalanx formation, but as the game gets closer and comes into view, the flanks begin to move out ahead, and the line assumes a crescent shape, the horns gradually getting closer to each other until they link up and the game is inside the line completely surrounded.

If there is a strong wind blowing, the horn on the windward side should ride by at a good distance from the game, or its scent might make the animal aware of its approach, and before it can be surrounded, the game will slip away. If the game becomes alarmed before the horns have had time to link up and should make a dash to avoid capture and escape through the gap between the horns, then the flank guards on both sides of the horns should move up more rapidly in column until they make contact. That is, they advance to the tips of the horns and fill up the gap between them, so that the game is caught back within the line of horsemen. After cutting off the game's escape route, the horns of the line make contact and then ride past one another, the right flank keeping to the inside and the left to the outside. With both flanks continuing their spiral movement, the game is gradually forced to the center, and that place, now surrounded by the line of horsemen, is constricted until after four or more full circles have been made the whole circumference is one or two miles. The game can then be quickly reached, and the space will be large enough for the archers to fire without hurting one another.

When the circle has been closed in the manner described, some
foot soldiers, if they are present, carrying shields, should be brought
inside that closed circle on foot and stationed with their shields
joined together in front of the horsemen. This should prevent
smaller animals likely to be surrounded from taking advantage of the
cramped quarters and slipping away through the legs of the horses. If
there are no infantry present, take some horsemen from the outer
circle of the formation and have them line up as just described.

After that, the general should appoint suitable officers or soldiers
to shoot the game from horseback. Outside of those appointed by
the general, nobody should dare ride in on the game. If the hour is
late, the space inside the circle may be further reduced by having the
foot soldiers link shield to shield to a certain height, so the game can
almost be dispatched by hand.

When everything has been completed as described, if the catch is
worthwhile, it should be distributed equally among the tagmas, so
that the morale of the whole army may pick up as the men enjoy the
fruits of their common labor. If the catch is not worth anything, distribute it by lot. Some reward should be given to the scouts, or spies,
if their work was carefully done.

This formation may be used by an army moving out from its camp
expressly for this purpose and then returning, or it may be used
while on the march. For it is suitable not only when the animals have
been well observed beforehand, but even when, as is likely, they have
been startled unexpectedly by the army marching along. It resembles
the battle formation which the Scythians like to use, but it is a little
slower and more drawn out. In fact, troops trying to use this formation for the first time should not put it to the test right away in an
actual hunt. Owing to their probable inexperience, the resultant
mistakes, toil, and fatigue will tend to discredit this formation as useless. Instead, first designate a few cavalrymen to represent the game,
so that the main body may use them to judge their distances and
easily come to learn the circling movements.

There is another method of conducting a hunt which we believe is
quicker and easier, and which can be done even by a small contingent
of horsemen, especially if the animals have been marked out beforehand. The day before the hunt the army is divided into five contingents, a third, a fourth, and a twelfth of the force. The third becomes
the center contingent, the two fourths the flank contingents, and the
two twelfths the flank guards. As the army, now, approaches the
selected point, as already described, the scouts, acting as guides, and

doing their best in the time allotted, work to bring the game around to opposite the center contingent and not to the sides. The center division is first drawn up in phalanx form, that is, along the mouth or front. Behind it comes the left division with its flank guards on its left flank a little to the rear. Following it is the right contingent likewise with its flank guards on its right and to the rear. The scouts go on ahead, taking position on the edges of the flank divisions, where the flank guards are drawn up. The center division halts in line, while the others pass by its flanks evenly toward the game. As soon as the other divisions have moved up, the center goes along without a break. The result is that the whole formation becomes like one of the regular orders of battle, the one with flanks advanced. They continue marching to the point where the horns pass the game, which is now on their inside. With the game now almost surrounded, the flank guards move in from both sides in a column, increase their gait, and make contact with each other, closing the fourth side, so that the whole formation now becomes like a rectangular brick. With the game completely surrounded, the horsemen on all four sides tighten or close in. The horsemen on the flanks close in on the flank guards, with those of the center following along. In like manner the flank guards tighten their own ranks, and the men on the flanks maneuver, so that in their section there will be no gap through which the game might escape. When the lines have been properly closed, a suitable place is selected where the game thus surrounded may be shot down. Maintaining good, close order, two sides then halt. The other two close in or increase depth, advancing toward one another until they are three or four bowshots apart. The other sides adapt their movements, as we have several times remarked, and close in with them on their flanks. As the place where the game is becomes more constricted, they then proceed, as mentioned above, to shooting it. This formation can be organized immediately upon leaving camp. The center contingent marches in front, as noted, and the other two follow along behind until near the game. When the army finds a protected place about three or four miles from the game, the maneuver described above may begin.

There is one other method which can be carried out by an even smaller number of horsemen, one which the Scythians like to use. The horsemen are divided into squads of five or ten men each, mostly archers. These divide up among themselves the territory outside where the game is. When the game is started, the men in their own areas advance and on getting close to it, as best they can, they begin shooting. This method, however, although providing more excitement and training for the individual because of all the riding about can be dangerous for the younger soldiers, can tire out the horses, and can lead to mistakes.

Ω Ω Ω Ω Ω Ω Ω Ω Ω Ω Ω Ω Ω Ω Ω Ω Ω Ω Ω Ω
Ω Ω Ω Ω Ω Ω Ω Ω Ω Ω Ω Ω Ω Ω Ω Ω Ω Ω Ω Ω

·GLOSSARY·

Alans: a nomadic people dwelling in the steppes north of the Black Sea.

Antes: a people, probably Slavic, living northeast of the Balkans in what is now the Ukraine.

arithmos: (*numerus*) a number of troops, often the same as a tagma, about three hundred men.

assault troops: (*cursores*) troops in open or extended order.

Avars: a nomadic people from central Asia who established a sort of empire in east central Europe.

ballista: a projectile-firing torsion weapon, like a large bow, usually operated by two or more soldiers.

bandon: a flag or standard, also a unit of about three hundred troops.

bowshot: flight range was about 300 meters, while target range was about 133 meters. Probably the latter is meant in the *Strategikon*. See Book II, n. 3.

bucellary troops: originally soldiers hired by private individuals, but who came to be a division of the regular army.

caltrop: metal objects with three or four protruding spikes designed to trip up horses.

cape bearer: an orderly.

chiliarch: commander of a thousand, equivalent to moirarch or duke.

chiliarchy: literally, unit of a thousand, but it came to include more troops and was equivalent to a moira.

count: commander of a bandon.

defenders: (*defensores*) troops in close or compact order.

dekarch: leader of ten soldiers.

dekarchy: squad of about ten soldiers.

division: body of troops, here equivalent to a meros, six to seven thousand soldiers.

171

draconarius: bearer of the dragon symbol, which was no longer in use by the sixth century. His function at this time is not known.

droungos: (*globus*) a body of troops massed together in irregular formation as for an ambush or surprise attack.

duke: commander of a moira, same as moirarch.

eagle bearer: an aide-de-camp or orderly.

federate troops: (*Federati*) originally allied tribes serving in the army in accord with a treaty, but by the sixth century they formed a sort of foreign legion in the regular army.

file: a line or squad of soldiers, from front to rear about ten men for cavalry, sixteen for infantry.

file leader: first man in a file, same as dekarch.

foulkon: a body of troops in very close order, sometimes forming a solid wall with shields overlapping and spear points sticking out.

general: (*strategos*) commander of an entire army.

Goths: a Germanic people who lived north of the Danube until the fourth century before migrating to the West. Large numbers of them served in the Roman army.

hekatontarch: commander of a hundred soldiers.

hekatontarchy: unit of about a hundred soldiers.

Herules: Germanic people who served as mercenaries for the Romans in the fifth and sixth centuries.

ilarch: the first hekatontarch, second in command to the count of a bandon.

Illyrikians: a body of troops which at one time had been stationed in Syria and Palestine.

lieutenant general: (*hypostrategos*) second in command of the entire army.

merarch: commander of a meros.

meros: division, unit composed of three moiras, approximately six to seven thousand men.

moira: unit composed of three bandons, one to two thousand men.

moirarch: commander of a moira, also called duke.

nomisma: a coin, legal tender of unspecified denomination.

Optimates: a body of troops, probably formed around the end of the third century.

outflankers: troops assigned to envelop the enemy wings or flanks.

pentarch: leader of five soldiers.

phalanx: a square or rectangular formation of an unspecified number of troops.

promachos: first line of troops in battle formation.

quartering parties: troops assigned to reconnoiter ahead of the army and to select camp sites.

172

schola: a military unit, originally part of the imperial guard.

Scythian: a general term used to designate the nomadic tribes north of the Black Sea and through central Asia.

Slavs: The Slavs here described lived along the lower Danube in what is now Rumania.

spatharios: an aide.

squad: unit of about ten soldiers, same as dekarchy.

stratelates: another name for merarch.

strator: an aide.

support: second line of soldiers in battle formation.

tagma: a formation of troops, in the *Strategikon* generally equivalent to bandon, about three hundred troops.

taxiarch: name given to the moirarch or commander of one to two thousand troops in the Optimates corps.

tetrarch: leader of four soldiers.

tribune: commander of a bandon, equivalent to count.

Trisagion: designates both the threefold "holy" beginning the eucharistic canon and the hymn: "Holy God, holy strong one, holy immortal one, have mercy on us."

Turks: at this time these would be the western Turks, north of Persia and to the east of the Black Sea.

Vexillation: originally a small detachment of troops, but by the sixth century a regular army division.

INDEX